GW01239578

The Classic Guide to TENNIS

The
Classic Guide
to
TENNIS

JOHN MOYER HEATHCOTE

AMBERLEY

Originally published in 1890
This edition first published 2014

Amberley Publishing
The Hill, Stroud, Gloucestershire, GL5 4EP
www.amberley-books.com

ISBN 978 1 4456 4118 8 (print)
ISBN 978 1 4456 4130 0 (ebook)

British Library Cataloguing in Publication Data.
A catalogue record for this book is available from the British Library.

Typesetting by Amberley Publishing.
Printed in Great Britain.

Contents

Introduction

The modern game of tennis evolved in the late nineteenth century. The history of the sport can be traced back to twelfth-century France and a game called *jeu de paume* (game of the palm), and racquets were first introduced in the sixteenth century. However, it was not until the period between 1859 and 1865 that 'lawn tennis' – the rules we know today – was developed by Harry Gem and Augorio Perera in Birmingham. This combined the elements of several other games, including racquets and pelota. In 1872, they founded the first tennis club in the world in Leamington Spa.

The predecessor to lawn tennis was a similar racquet sport called 'real tennis', and during most of the nineteenth century the term 'tennis' actually referred to this. 'Real tennis' is dealt with in chapters 1–5 of this book, while 'lawn tennis' is covered in chapters 6–18. Today, tennis is a multi-billion-pound industry, played at a professional level all over the world and watched by millions of people. There are now four international Grand Slam tournaments (the Wimbledon Championships, Australian Open, French Open and US Open), organised and regulated by the International Tennis Federation, and numerous other high-profile tournaments throughout the world, including the Davis Cup, a competition that was formed in 1900.

The world's oldest tennis tournament, the Wimbledon Championships, was first played in London in 1877. These Championships culminated in a debate on how to standardise the rules of the sport as it evolved. John Moyer Heathcote was one of the committee that devised the original standardised rules of lawn tennis, which remain almost unchanged to this day. He is credited with inventing the cloth covering for the tennis ball, which was previously comprised of vulcanised rubber. He played 'real tennis' for several years between 1856 and 1866, and won the gold prize from Marylebone Cricket Club for amateur tennis for fifteen years running, and was considered the amateur real tennis champion until 1882. He was thought to be one of the best players in the world at the time.

Heathcote died in 1912. A veteran of the tennis court, he lived in a time of revolution for the sport of tennis, and had an incredible impact on the formation of the modern game. Later in his life he set down much of the knowledge and expertise he had accumulated over his long career in a volume entitled *Tennis, Lawn Tennis, Rackets & Fives*, one of the very first 'manuals' of the sport, in 1890. The *Classic Guide to Tennis* is a remastered version of this seminal work. It includes many contemporary illustrations, and instructs the budding tennis player in how to become a true master of the game.

The Editor

1

The Paleontology of Ball Games

The writer on this subject may cultivate brevity easily enough, but the dearth of trustworthy information will necessarily leave him and his readers somewhat in the dark. We may, however, assume as probable that in the very earliest ages a ball was, as it is now, a favourite toy with children and a means of recreation to athletes of both sexes.

There is no allusion in Hebrew Scriptures to any pastime of this or any other character, nor have I been able to learn that Assyrian inscriptions have thrown any light on the subject; but the excavations at Gurob (a village about sixty miles south of Cairo), by Mr Flinders Petrie, have brought light implements for recreation that unquestionably belong to the period of the twelfth dynasty, and must therefore have been in existence for more than 4,000 years. In this place were found balls made of leather, and some also made of wood; the former are now rather battered and out of shape, but I saw one wooden ball in Mr Petrie's collection, an almost perfect sphere about the size of a billiard ball. But even more interest may be attached to the discovery of several tip cats, bearing a close resemblance to the disagreeable missile so dear to the London gamin, for these bear silent witness to the primeval existence of a game in which force is applied and motion imparted to a projectile by an implement of some sort.

The invention of the ball in Europe is attributed by Herodotus to the Lydians in the reign of Atys. We read that Anagalla, a native of Corcyra, presented a ball to Nausicaa, the daughter of Alcinous, King of Phaeacia, and the pastimes of that lady and her attendants are too well known to require comment. Theodor Panofka tells us that astragali and ball were the popular pastimes of the age, and that the latter was a favourite amusement of the gods. Every schoolboy knows that Maecenas played at ball at Capua, and that Virgil and Horace did not. Pilicrepi, ball players, or jugglers, are mentioned in one of the political inscriptions of Pompeii. We are told that Augustus used to play at ball, and that Pliny's friend Spurinna exercised himself in some such game with a view of warding off old age, and the allusions to a sphaeristerium, or arena for play, and to various games – follis, trigonalis, paganica and harpastum – in Pliny, Ovid, Martial, Horace, Plautus, and Propertius, prove the popularity of some such pastime in the classic ages. Becker tells us that the last mentioned of these games was a rough and violent one, but it is worthy of notice because it is the earliest example of a sphaeromachia, or game in which sides were formed, as appears by the terms used by Galen: emulation (φιλοτιμια), generalship (στρατηγια); and positions lost and won – φαινινδα, φενινδα, εφετινδα and πεννις. In Gilbert Wakefield's notes on Pope's translation of Homer's *Odyssey* we are told that the Lacedaemonians used to play Harpastum, then known by the names φαινινδα, φενινδα, εφετινδα and φεννις. If philological research could but find precedent for the interchange of φ and τ we should have a remarkable instance of the revival – I can hardly say survival – of the fittest designation for our game.

But there is little or no evidence to show whether these pastimes were games in the modern acceptance of the word, or were gymnastic exercises in which young athletes indulged with a view of acquiring muscular strength and grace of movement, nor is it possible to trace in them any affinity to tennis. It may, however, be interesting to note a few expressions and allusions that suggest that throwing and returning a ball may have been an element of some of these exercises.

L. Becq de Fouquières tells us that the following terms were frequently used: ριπτειν, βαλλειν, αφιεναι, ανταφιεναι, πεμπειν, μροπεμπειω, and αντιπεμπειν. That sides may have been formed, and the players opposed to one another, may perhaps be inferred from a passage in the writings of the Byzantine historian Pollux quoted by him : '*Le vaincu était appelé âne* (ονος) *et faisait tout ce qui lui était commandé; le vainqueur était nommé roi* (βασιλευς), *et ordonnait*'. No light is thrown on these expressions in Grecian history, but we read,

> '*Parmi les peintures égyptiennes de Beni-Hassan il en est une particuliérement curieuse qui donne raison à notre hypothèse. Deux femmes, placées à quelque distance l'une de l'autre, sont montées sur deux de leurs compagnes, et jouent à la balle. On doit reconnaître là un jeu qu'on pratique encore de nos jours. Plusieurs joueurs montés sur le dos de leurs camarades se lancent la balle de l'un à l'autre. Celui qui la laisse échapper devient à son tour le porteur.*'

Plautus uses the terms *datores* and *factores*; 'stroke' and 'return' are forcibly suggested by *datatim ludere, remittere, repercutere, expulsare, geminare*, and the following expressive line, '*Et non sperato fugientem reddere gestu*', a which must appeal to the heart of a tennis player, and recall to his mind the supreme effort that enabled him to make an unexpected return.

The literature of ball games ceases soon after the Christian era, but as all literature declined at this age, it is not surprising that we have little or no information over many centuries. It is reasonable to suppose that some ball games continued to be popular in Italy, and were thus introduced by Roman soldiers into Gaul and Spain, and that these were the germs from which longue paume, pallone, and other kindred exercises, the prototypes of tennis, derived their origin.

Handball, or longue paume, as it was called in the Middle Ages, was played in Italy and France in the parks or *fosses* of the chateaux, or in any uncovered arenas that could be found suitable for the purpose.

Strutt gives representations of what he calls balloon and handball taken from MSS of the fourteenth century. The picture on page 101 is a facsimile of one of these. Here we see a player just about to strike a pallone, or large ball, with the palm of his hand. Near him stands a man who is apparently an attendant or instructor, and on the opposite side of the inter-columnar ornament are two players ready to receive and return the ball.

We are frequently reminded that longue paume was the sport of kings and nobles. Villaret tells us that the death of Louis X was caused by a chill caught when playing in the forest of Vincennes in 1316. In 1399, the game was played for the amusement of Charles VI at the chateau of Creil-sur-Oise. Brantome says of Charles IX that 'when it was fine he was always out of doors, either campaigning or in action, or playing *la paume*, and particularly *la longue paume*, of which he was very fond'.

We have every reason to believe that this, the oldest of French ball games, was practised continuously through many centuries, in the course of which the substitution of an implement for the hand, the use of improved balls, and the institution of 'chases' invested the pastime with constantly increasing interest. This interest, however, began to wane in the early part of this century. There was an arena for play in the Champs Llysees in 1820, and the headquarters of Longue Paume in Paris were subsequently removed to the Luxembourg Gardens, where the game was played in 1867. But by this time it had lost its popular character, and is now seldom if ever played.

Pallone, the Olympic game, or game of giants, as it has been called, owes its origin to some early Roman ball game. Its growth was contemporary with that of Longue Paume, but we have no evidence to show that one was derived from the other, or even that they had a common ancestor. The ball, which may have resembled the Roman follis, was the earliest of which we have any record made of the bladder of some animal covered with leather and inflated with air, and probably did not differ very much from those now in use. The modern ball is 5 inches in diameter; it is hollow, and has a double coat of strong cowhide. In this covering is a small hole furnished with a valve, which allows air to be driven into the ball by a force pump and prevents its escape.

The elasticity thus imparted to the ball is so great that if dropped on to a hard floor it will rebound to within a few inches from the point from which it fell. The hand that sufficed for the cruder ball of early times gave place to a *scanno* or wooden club, or to a *bracciale*, a cylindrical gauntlet covered with blunt spikes, worn on the hand and wrist. Dr A. Fisher has written an interesting work on ancient and modern pallone, to which the reader who seeks further information is referred. In his description of the game as played in 1822 at Bologna, he says that a 'pallone' may be driven 100 yards. This is probably no exaggeration, for at an exhibition of Pallone given at the Queen's

Club, West Kensington, on Easter Monday 1889, some Italian players from Alva, near Turin, illustrated the wonderful propelling power of a weapon so clumsy in appearance, yet so effective in execution, as a bracciale.

There was, until recently, a court in Florence near the Porta San Gallo, and an oil painting by Raphael Sorbi, a Florentine artist, that gave a good representation of six players engaged three a side in the game as played in the last century. This court is now pulled down, as are many others in Italy, and the game is now falling into disuse.

Another exercise, probably of great antiquity, is still practised in Northern France and Belgium, and is known as *Jeu de balle au tamis*. This game, as described to me by an English gentleman who witnessed its performance at Dinant on the Meuse, is played in a vast arena, about 120 yards in length, by twelve players, six on each side. The ball is small and inelastic, covered with white leather; the implement with which it is struck is a glove, to the palm of which is attached a strong piece of leather, as hard as wood, which presents to the ball a concave surface about 8 inches in length and 6 inches in breadth.

The tamis is used only in the delivery of the 'service'; it resembles a segment of a drum, and the horsehair of which it is formed is sufficiently elastic to enable the server to throw the ball on to its surface and strike it in its rebound. Little or no 'return' is possible when such implements as these are employed, but the establishment of and defence of 'chases' is an interesting feature in this game.

Another variety of la paume was, and still is, played in the Basque provinces, and is known by the name of *Jugar al blé*. It is described by a writer, who evidently has observed the game, as played at St Jean de Luz with 'a spoon-shaped basket or shield', called a *schistera*. This game, which is also called *Pelote au Rebot*, is usually played in the open air, but it is also well adapted to modern tennis courts. I had an opportunity of witnessing in 1867 an exposition of this interesting and unique pastime by four of the best players from the Basque provinces in the tennis court at Paris. The schistera they used was made of wickerwork, rather more than 2 feet in length, shaped like a curved canoe or basket. With this implement they caught and threw, rather than struck the ball, and their accuracy in playing for, and skill in defending, the openings were remarkable. The game was scored as at tennis in every respect; the balls were larger and heavier than tennis balls but resembled them in appearance.

That the above mentioned games had some affinity to modern tennis is sufficiently obvious, for the principle of 'stroke' and 'return' of a ball over a line marked in the arena for play by sides opposed to one another is common to them all, but there are also traditions of other ball games played in every quarter of the globe with an implement that might in courtesy be called a racket.

A game somewhat similar to lacrosse was played by the Chippeways, and the Mingrelians in Georgia indulged in a pastime that was not unlike modern polo. Byzantine authors mention a similar game called τζυκανιστηριον, in which, says Johannes Cinnamus, who lived around AD 1153, an implement with a broad curved end (καμπη), furnished with a network of catgut, was used. From this game was derived a similar exercise in Languedoc called *chicane*, described in Fosbrooke's *Encyclopaedia of Antiquities*, in which the implement with which the ball was struck was a sort of mallet. But the relation of these games to tennis is so remote that their investigation will be less interesting than that of the seven ages, or rather centuries, during the course of which the beautiful game known by the name of tennis was developed and brought by degrees to that perfect state in which we now find it.

In the course of these seven ages, its very name has undergone repeated changes, and no etymological research has satisfactorily solved the question why the game is so called in England. It has been suggested that the word may have been derived from Tennois or Sennois, in the district of Champagne in France, where it was said that the game was played, or from the French word *tenez*, which might have been used by the server to his opponent; but it is scarcely probable that our ancestors should have sought a French origin for a game which was known on the Continent as la paume. Skeat suggests *tænia* (Gr. ταινια), a fillet or band. This might bean equivalent for the rope or fringe over which the ball was played in the early days of the *giuoco della corda*. Others maintain that the game was first called 'tennes' because five competitors on each side were engaged in the exercise, and this contention is at least as satisfactory as any other. But, as guesses are not permissible in philology, it will be safer to leave tennis in the class of words whose derivation is unknown.

2

The History of the Court, Racket, and Ball

In the first age of tennis, the thirteenth century, the game was, in France, as far as we know, played only in unenclosed spaces, but so great was its popularity in the provinces, that early in the fourteenth century it was adopted in many towns as a means of recreation and exercise. It may easily be supposed that the difficulty of securing suitable arenas for play would be considerable, and this difficulty may have suggested the use of spaces surrounded by walls, or of edifices constructed for this special purpose, which, about that time, became known by the name of *tripots*. Why they were so called is a matter of conjecture. Etymologists have suggested no better derivation than *tripudiation* (active motion), but this is a matter of small moment, as the word is not now in use, French courts being always called *jeux*. Charles V was probably the pioneer of this improvement on the primeval game. Mr Marshall tells us that he had a court at the Louvre, which, according to M. de Clarac, occupied two entire storeys of the palace. He had another at his Hotel de Beautrellis, the magnificent *dependance* of the Hotel St Paul, which existed until 1552. This court was 87 feet in length, the French foot being about ¾ inch longer than the English measure of that name. This king, with an exclusiveness that would scarcely be tolerated in modern times, issued an edict prohibiting all games within his dominions, but early in the third age of tennis, or the fifteenth century, we hear of the erection of more courts in Paris, of which the most important was the tripot in the Rue Grenier Saint Lazare, called Le Petit Temple.

In this court, Margot, a young woman from the province of Hainault, was accustomed to display her skill, which was said to rival that of all except the very best players.

Tennis was still more universally encouraged in its fourth age, the sixteenth century. Francois I built another court in the Louvre, which is shown on page 101. In this court, Henri II, a really fine player, who might probably have carried off the *eteuf d'argent*, the insignia of championship, had he cared to enter the lists, used to play. At this time, there were two kinds of tripots, or jeux, as they were by this time called: the *jeu à dedans*, which closely resembled a modern tennis court, and the *jeu quarré*. From the latter the *dedans*, the 'end penthouse', on the 'service side', and the 'tambour' were absent; the 'winning hazards' were *le trou*, an 'opening', 16 square inches (French), opposite the 'grille'; *l'ais*, an upright board, 9-foot high, 1-foot wide, in the other corner of the same court, and *la lune*, a small, round opening, high up in the end wall on both sides of the court. The existence of the 'hazard' cannot have been of long duration, for it could not have been overlooked by De Garsault, who, in 1767, wrote a complete account of every detail of a tennis court, and as there is no reference to any such opening in his work, its use had probably by that time been abandoned.

Little is known of the origin of the 'tambour', or why it is so called. It is probable that it may have been an excrescence erected for the purpose of fulfilling the conditions of a hazard, and that it was made of wood, or some material whose resonance may have suggested the name. It is much more likely that all the above mentioned hazards were designed for the purpose of introducing variety into the play, and preventing undue advantage from accruing to the occupier of the service side, or hazard side, than being the result of the accidental configuration of courts of monasteries – a theory that has been propounded, but which cannot be supported by evidence.

We have testimony of the extraordinary popularity of la paume in Paris in a letter written by Lippomano, the Venetian ambassador, in which he says, 'There were more than 1,800 Tennis courts in various parts of the town of Paris'. Probably, however, most of these were merely uncovered spaces in which some ball exercise could be held. In the fifteenth century, there was a court at Windsor Castle, a representation of which is given on page 102. 'This is a facsimile of a view taken by John Norden in 1607, showing an uncovered court with a line or cord stretched across the centre, and a representation of a racket and some balls lying on the floor'. There is evidence of a covered court at Richmond in *Letters and Papers, Foreign and Domestic, of the Reign of Henry VIII*, arranged and catalogued by J. S. Brewer, 1519: 'Wages due Lady Day for ceiling the Tennis court at Richmond, and other places, 200*l*'. We also hear of a court at Greenwich, of another at Oxford, and of fourteen courts in London. The dimensions of these were less than those of the *jeu à dedans* at the Louvre, the largest being only 84 feet in length and 22 feet in breadth.

But the most interesting event of this age of tennis was the erection of the court at Hampton Court, because, although subsequently altered and partially rebuilt, it is the oldest court now extant in this country. We are told in the Annals:

> This court was built by Henry VIII after the year 1526, when Wolsey surrendered to him the lease of the Palace; for it is evident that at least the upper, if not also the lower, part of the wall is of later date than what remains elsewhere of Wolsey's building at Hampton Court, but is yet anterior to Wren's alteration of the garden front. Hollar fortunately sketched a view of this front as Henry VIII finished it, and as it remained until the time of Wren. This drawing has been preserved by the engraving of J. Pye (made for the Society of Antiquaries), a large oblong folio, which shows the tennis court, with the covered passage by which the King, it is said, used to pass from it to his apartment.

The picture on page 102 is a reproduction of this sketch.

In the fifth age, the seventeenth century, the game was no less popular than it had previously been. In 1614, there were two courts at the Palace of Fontainebleau. The image on page 103 is an accurate copy of a bird's-eye view entitled 'Portrait de la maison royale de Fontaine Belleau'. The number 8 indicates the position of the two courts, which form part of a block of buildings in the left corner of the Cour du Cheval Blanc. The image on page 103 shows the position of the modern court, on a site not far from that of the ancient building. The beauty of the architectural surroundings, and its own unobtrusive and harmonious character, offer to the eye of an artist a more picturesque scene than is usually presented by a combination of such utilitarian objects – a tennis court and a gas lamp. In 1657, the Dutch ambassador ascertained that there were 114 regular tripots in Paris, and in 1686, the court at Versailles, known to every student of the history of the French Revolution, was commenced and completed; not, however, until after Louis XIV, who had in his youth been fond of tennis, had ceased to reside in the palace.

Contemporary history in England teaches us that Charles I, while Duke of York, began to play tennis, and that in 1610, his account for rackets, balls, and other necessaries, amounted to 20s. In 1619, we hear of his making an appointment to play in the court at St James's Palace at 6 a.m., and his love of the game continued after he had ascended the throne. Although the stern realities of the Rebellion and the troubled times of the Commonwealth hindered its further development, the numerous references made to tennis in *Pepys's Diary* show that it reasserted its popularity in the reign of the Merry Monarch, who used to frequently play in the court in James Street, Haymarket, the erection of which enhances the interest that is attached to the records of that century. This court has been the theatre of important matches and first-class play, and has been the resort of distinguished lovers of the game to a greater extent than any other court in the world; and lovers of tennis cannot but deplore the inexorable laws of supply and demand that so enhanced the value of land in the metropolis that the maintenance of this court could no longer be a financial success, and regretfully recall to mind the conversion of a building so rich in interesting associations into the warehouse of an army clothier in 1866.

Although I had separated the aeon of tennis into seven ages, or centuries, I had no intention of parodying Shakespeare's series of metaphors; but it is remarkable that in the sixth age we first hear of 'spectacles on nose', worn by the celebrated Masson, and that the number of courts was a world too wide for the shrunken company of players and frequenters. In the eighteenth century, many of the old tripots were pulled down, others were converted into theatres, and in

1780, we are told that at the most there remained but thirteen of the 114 that had been in existence two centuries before that time.

In our own country, the game was beginning to lose its popular character, although still played by the higher classes of society. Many old courts were abandoned or destroyed, and we hear of the construction of three only in the latter half of the century: the Duke of Richmond's at Goodwood; the Duke of Bedford's at Woburn; and the court in Tennis Court Road, Cambridge, erected in 1734, recently pulled down and replaced by the new buildings of Pembroke College.

There is, however, no probability of the last age of this eventful history passing into mere oblivion, for the nineteenth century has witnessed a renewed and constantly increasing enthusiasm for tennis, shown by the number of courts built by public and private enterprise, on improved lines, and equipped with modern requirements, and by the interest taken in all important matches.

On the Continent, although it has witnessed the closing, in 1839, of the court in the Rue Mazarine in Paris, its chronicles record the construction, in 1840, and existence, until it was removed to make room for the new opera house, of the excellent court in the Passage Sandrie; the erection of two courts now standing in the Terrasse des Feuillants, in the Jardin des Tuileries; the reopening of the court at Bordeaux; and the construction of courts at Deauville, Cannes and Pau. Three have been recently erected in America, Melbourne and Tasmania; and in our own country, while three only have been pulled down – one at Cambridge and two at Prince's Club – the list has been augmented by no less than thirty constructed since the beginning of this century, and it may be predicted with confidence that before its close we shall have seen the completion of many more courts in response to the ever-increasing requirements of our young athletes.

The following is a list of courts now existing in this country:

Four in London – one at Lord's, two at the Queen's Club, West Kensington, and one at Prince's Club, Knightsbridge.
One at Hampton Court.
Two at Cambridge.
One at Oxford.

One at Leamington.
One at Brighton.
One at Manchester.
The Duke of Richmond's at Goodwood.
The Duke of Bedford's at Woburn.
The Duke of Wellington's at Strathfieldsaye.
The Duke of Fife's at East Sheen.
The Marquis of Salisbury's at Hatfield.
The Earl of Craven's at Coombe Abbey.
Lord Windsor's at Hewell Grange.
Lord Leconfield's at Petworth.
Lord Brougham's at Brougham Hall.
Lord Wimborne's at Canford.
Sir George Prescott's at Theobalds.
Sir T. Hesketh's at Easton Neston.
Sir E. Loder's at Whittlebury.
Mr Cazalet's at Fairlawn.
Mr Gundry's at Bridport.
Sir E. Guinness's in Dublin.
Mr Orehardson's at Westgate-on-Sea.
Mr McClean's at Rustall, Tunbridge Wells.

With the exception of the twin courts at the Queen's Club, which were designed by one architect and erected by one builder at the same time, on the same lines, and with similar materials, no two courts are exactly alike, but it will be generally admitted that Lord Leconfield's court at Petworth is the fastest in England, while the Brighton court is the slowest, and that the courts at the Queen's Club, Manchester, Mr Gundry's, the court built by the late Sir R. Coder, Mr Cazalet's, and the newly erected court at Prince's Club, most nearly approach perfection with regard to dimensions, light, and relative 'pace' of walls and floor.

It may be interesting to compare the salient features of seven typical courts, which include the largest courts in existence, Fontainebleau, Hampton Court, and Lord's; the smallest, Brougham and Oxford; and two that may be cited as perfect models, Whittlebury and Manchester.

A detailed account of the characteristics of these tennis courts would occupy too much space, but brief mention must be made of the charming and unique court erected in 1875, by Mr W. Q. Orchardson, R.A., at Westgate-on-Sea. The floor, which is 90ft 6in. in length, 30ft 2in. in breadth, is made of Portland cement, and is laid on 6in. of concrete, which rests on the chalk soil. The main wall, which is 18ft high, batteries and end walls below the penthouse, are made of brick, and are covered with Portland cement. The walls above the penthouse are the same height as the main wall, and are formed with boards laid longitudinally. The penthouse is supported by light posts, around which are trained honeysuckle, Virginia creeper and Banksia roses, forming an ornamental trellised arcade outside the court. There is no roof, but wire netting 8ft high, carried round the entire court, is sufficient to prevent the loss of balls. It might be imprudent to erect such a court on a clay soil, or in a situation where the rainfall is excessive, but anyone who wishes for this valuable adjunct to a country house will find that he can gratify his ambition without being called on to spend more than one-fourth of the cost of a fully equipped court, and that, although precluded from play on damp or rainy days, he will fully appreciate the charm of exercise *sub jove*. The picture on page 104 shows this court as seen from the dedans.

Some interest may be attached to the structure at Rustall, as it is more suggestive of the game played by our ancestors in the sixteenth century than any modern building, and also because it is the only court in England where use is made of black balls, as was formerly the custom in Spain. It was recently built by Mr McClean as an arena for long fives, and although it lacks the refinement and interest of tennis, owing to the absence of chase lines, it affords scope for an excellent game, with which any tennis player can readily make himself familiar. This court is perfectly symmetrical, the service side and the hazard side being similar in every respect. The walls and floor are of Portland cement, and a small penthouse of the same material is taken round the entire structure. The court is entered from a gallery at the net, and there is a corresponding gallery in the opposite main wall; but these openings are 'out of court'. There are no dedans, grille, or tambour; the only hazards are two openings, 3 feet square, in the centre of each end wall below the penthouse. It was not designed in imitation of any past or present court, but in many particulars it bears some resemblance to the representations we have of the *jenx quarres* of earlier ages.

Having thus briefly traced the outline of the history of the court, I will here introduce a paper by Mr W. C. Marshall, which enters fully on the most suitable aspect for a tennis court, on the best building materials and on the systems of lighting and ventilation that he considers to be most satisfactory, and throws light on that most difficult problem, the relative pace of walls and floor. These details merit the attention of all who are interested in the past or the future construction of a tennis court.

The Court

Aspect – If practicable, a tennis court should stand east and west, with the dedans at the east end. This position gives least glare from the skylights, and places the main wall, in which it is desirable to have windows, on the north side.

The Floor – Marble, various freestones and cement, have been used for the floor of a tennis court. Marble is costly, and said to become slippery. Sandstones are all more or less liable to flake. It is difficult to make cement quite uniform in character, and the kind of elasticity it possesses is less suitable to the game of tennis than to that of rackets.

The best material is a fine, uniform limestone, such as the blue lias used at Lord's, the Queen's Club, and the new Prince's Club courts.

Caen stone also makes a very good floor. Though a soft stone, it hardens with time, and stands the wear well. It is easy to lay with a close joint, but is light in colour, and, in this country, more costly than lias; it has been employed at the courts built for the Duke of Fife at Sheen, and for the Trinity and Clare Club at Cambridge. With the exception of black marble and some sandstones, no natural stone is dark enough, but requires to be stained.

At the Queen's Club the floors were treated alternately with solutions of permanganate of potash and manganese sulphate; this double application causes manganese to be deposited in the stone to whatever depth the solutions penetrate – in the instance mentioned to about ¹⁄₁₆ inch – and forms a quite permanent dark brown dye to that depth. This method is not injurious to the stone, and is in every way preferable to the slippery and evil-smelling compound of bullock's blood and black formerly used.

Walls – Whether the walls are built of brick or stone will depend on local considerations; in any case they must be coated about 1 inch thick with Portland cement. The surface should not be quite as smooth as the plasterer is able to work it; but as the more the cement is worked the harder and better it becomes, it is best to have it brought to a smooth face and then lightly brushed over, by which means a slight uniform roughness is obtained.

The walls require colouring, and various plans have been tried. Distemper comes off and dirties the balls; oil paint, japan and similar substances stop the suction of the cement, and to some extent prevent it from absorbing condensed moisture, and so cause what is generally called 'sweating' of the walls; moreover, paint cannot be used on cement until it is twelve months old. The difficulty in finding a satisfactory colouring material for the walls has led to the use of coloured cement, and it is interesting to note that the remains of the walls of the old court at Easton Neston were finished in very hard, black cement about an ¹⁄₈ inch thick. Recently, in Mr Gundry's court lamp black, and in the Queen's Club courts vegetable black, have been used successfully for this purpose. Manganese black is a better dye, interfering less with the setting of the cement. Any colouring matter, however, diminishes to some extent the strength of the cement.

The battery walls should be built of brickwork with cement mortar, and cemented in the same way as the rest of the walls. In some courts, the end walls and tambour are faced with stone. Unless very well fixed the stones are liable to be shaken, and when well built, as at Manchester, they are somewhat too lively.

The cement should be taken over the sills of galleries and round the sides of all openings, slightly rounded on the edge. If wood sills are used, the joint between the cement and wood is apt to break away.

In connection with the floor and walls the question naturally arises: What constitutes a fast court? This is not very easy to answer, for the word 'fast' is apparently used to imply different things: either that the ball travels fast, or that the player has to strike or move fast. To satisfy the first definition, the floor and walls should be as smooth and elastic as possible. To satisfy the second, the floor and side walls should be smooth and inelastic, the back wall rough and elastic – the floor being the most important factor.

In considering this question, it must be borne in mind that the horizontal velocity of a ball is much greater than the vertical velocity, perhaps eight times as great on the average. A ball will come away quickest from a perfectly smooth and elastic floor. Inelasticity diminishes the vertical velocity, roughness the horizontal.

Inelasticity, therefore, does not materially diminish the pace of the ball, but it does diminish the time the ball is on the bound, which depends solely on the vertical component of the velocity. Hence, on an inelastic floor, the ball will travel nearly as fast as on an elastic one, but the bound will be shorter, and the time to strike less.

A rough floor, on the other hand, will diminish the velocity materially, but not at all affect the length of time on the bound.

The conditions are similar with regard to the side walls, except that inelasticity does not shorten the time of the bound, but causes the ball to keep nearer the walls, compelling the player to move further in order to reach it. In the case of the end walls, the conditions are reversed, as the pace at which the ball will come off from it depends almost entirely on the elasticity of the wall, while roughness will make a cut ball fall quicker, but will have little effect on one that is not cut.

The writer's view is that both the floor and walls should have a high degree of elasticity, which is to be attained by hardness and solidity, that the floor should be smooth but not polished, and the walls should have a slight degree of roughness sufficient to give full effect to cut and twist.

Lighting – There should always be ample skylights. In a smoky town, a width of 10 feet on either side of the ridge, supposing the roof is of the ordinary single-span description, will not be too much. Rough-rolled plate glass is the best for glazing; this cannot be bought in greater lengths than 8 feet, and it is better not to exceed 6. Whether the ordinary wood bars or one of the patent systems of glazing is used, it is essential to provide for carrying off any water condensed on the under surface of the glass.

The diffusion of light is assisted by the employment of light-coloured woodwork in the roof and ceiling. Windows in the main wall above the play line, although not essential, are valuable for lighting, as well as for ventilation. They should be glazed with ground glass to avoid the necessity of blinds.

It is better not to have any windows in the service wall, as they cause a shadow to be thrown under the side batteries.

The question of electric lighting has not as yet been tested. Gas has been tried, but the result was unsatisfactory. The problem of lighting a large room with black walls, and where all lights must be kept 30 feet from the floor, is a novel and difficult one, and it is hard to say what amount of light would be required.

The cost of a separate installation for such occasional use as would be required would be almost prohibitive; but where current could be laid on, it would be worthy of consideration. The cost, in addition to the original outlay, would probably be from 2–3s an hour.

Ventilation and Warming – The windows should be made to open easily and quickly; an outside gallery is generally provided for this purpose, and it is important the marker should have easy access to it.

Where there are no buildings adjoining, large hit-and-miss ventilators, of the description used in stables, can be put in the side wall and under the penthouse.

Roof ventilation is, of course, desirable, but the necessary gearing for opening and shutting any ventilators is expensive and often difficult to arrange.

Warming, except to a very moderate extent, is not required for the players, but a coil of hot water pipes will help to keep the court dry. It may be placed in a channel under the net covered with an iron grating, in the position of the trough usually formed to catch the balls.

Hot water pipes in the dedans are a comfort to spectators.

A system of ventilation, when all windows and other openings are closed – which, by slightly warming the floor and walls, effectually prevents condensation of moisture, a frequent cause of interference with play in the winter months – has been adopted at the Manchester and Queen's Club courts. The floor is carried by brick arches, and in the vaults are placed hot water pipes. The walls are built with a hollow space, up which the warm air escapes into the upper part of the court.

An extract flue of large size, in connection with the flue from the furnace, draws air from a grating under the net, and so provides for a complete circulation.

The amount of warming effected is slight, but sufficient, and in a public court such an arrangement is very desirable.

Penthouse – The roof of the penthouse should be covered with boards 1½ inch thick, or with two layers of inch boarding. The nosing, or plate forming the bandeau, should be of oak or some other hard wood.

Posts – The gallery posts should be as small as possible and are, therefore, better made of iron than wood. The hook to which the end of the net is attached should be sunk in the main wall.

Lines – The play line should be made of wood, whose resonance helps the marker to judge when a ball is out of play, a point which, from his position, it is often difficult for him to decide.

The bandeau, the chase lines and other lines, should be painted in subdued tints; light or staring colours catch the eye and are very distracting.

Cost – The expense of building varies greatly with time and place, but the cost of a well-appointed tennis court, exclusive of dressing rooms or any accommodation for a marker, may be roughly stated at 2,000*l.*

The Racket

Littré tells us that the oldest form of this word was *rachete*, or *rasquete*, and gives as a probable derivation, *racha*, old Latin for καρπος or ταρσος, the wrist or ankle. M. de Paulmy mentions the early use in Italy of a *racchetta*, and of a *raqueta* in Spain. The evolution of those words from 'retis', 'reticus', 'reticulum', 'reticulata' and 'retiquetta' has been offered as an alternative solution of this philological problem. It is probable that the Italians, when playing la paume, found that a glove was a useful protection to the hand, and when balls were made harder and heavier, that a thicker glove was required. The transition from the thick glove to a network of strings, and the adoption of the leverage afforded by the use of a handle, may have suggested to an ingenious inventor the prototype of the implement we now use. M. Edouard Fournier, describing a racket of the times of François I, says:

> *Ce précieux outil était un lacis de cordes croisées l'une sur l'autre, en façon de mailles et de rets, encadré dans un cadre de bois qui. s'emmanchait lui-meme d'un court et fort bâton ... Les dames de la cour de Catherine de Médicis arrangeaient leurs cheveux en les croisant par bandes, comme les raquettiers disposaient leurs cordes. C'était ce qu'on appelait la coiffure en raquettes: nous dirions aujourd'hui en nattes.*

From this we may infer that in the earlier form of this *precieux outil*, the hoop was strung diagonally, not with main strings, parallel to the handle and cross strings at right angles to them, and this inference is confirmed by an illustration of the court at the Louvre, by Scaino, dated 1555, in which there is a representation of a racket strung in this manner. The latest instance of a racket so strung occurs in a facsimile of a view of the interior of the 'Jeu de Paurne commun-jardin', bearing date 1701.

The French antiquary Pasquier tries to fix the date of its introduction into France, relating that he, when a young man, was informed by a person named Gastelier, then seventy-six years of age, who had been a great player in his youth, that within his, Gastelier's recollection, la paume had been played solely with the hand, some persons using it uncovered, some protecting it with a glove, and, subsequently, with a network of cords and tendons. As Pasquier was born in 1528, this conversation may have occurred about 1550, and suggests the probability of the general adoption of the racket in the waning of the fifteenth century.

We have evidence of a distinctive era in the history of the racket in a manuscript quoted by Mr Marshall, which, after describing the sports and pastimes provided for the amusement of Philip Archduke of Austria, King of Castile, when he was entertained by Henry VII at Windsor Castle, tells us that 'Both Kyngs went to the tennys playe, and the Kynge of Casteele played with the Rackete, and gave the Lord Marques (Dorset) XV'. From this we may infer that at the beginning of the sixteenth century, a racket was used by the foreigner, who was thus enabled to give points to his English opponent, who used the hand only.

At this period use was also made of a *battoir*, or battledore, made with parchment and furnished with a long handle when required for longue paume, with a shorter handle for courte paurne, or the game played in a tripot. That these battoirs were in great demand is shown by M. Fournier, who tells us that the makers, when the supply of parchment ran short, had been known to avail themselves of precious manuscripts, which they procured from persons who were ignorant of their value.

In support of this statement, he quotes the following passage from Colomies:

> *J'ai ouï dire à M. Chapelain qu'un de ses amis, homme de lettres, avait joué à la longue paume avec un battoir sur lequel se voyaient des fragments de quelques décades de Tite Live que nous n'avons pas, et que ces fragments venaient d'un apoticaire qui, ayant en don des religieuses de Fontevrault plusieurs volumes en parchemin du même auteur, les avait vendus par ignorance à un faiseur de raquettes.*

The picture on page 104 is taken from a work by Mitelli, an Italian artist who painted in Bologna in 1675. Although a mere sketch, it is evidently the work of a skilled draughtsman, and is probably an accurate representation of the racket used in those days.

The picture on page 105 shows the changes that were effected in the course of a century. We find that in De Garsault's time, 1767, the middle piece was used, and the racket, though wanting in finish, differed but slightly from a modern implement. What appears in the engraving to be a transverse rod is a wire bridle, in those days carried round the hoop, for the purpose of preventing loss of shape.

Picture no. 10 on p. 105 shows a racket such as we now use, which is as nearly perfect as is possible; indeed, its very perfection has been said by some players to have caused deterioration of the game of tennis, which has become so fast that the balance between activity and skill is less evenly adjusted than it was in the past. A new departure was made in or around 1857. Before that time the cross strings were looped round the main strings, but it was found that when these were threaded through them, the racket so strung would drive the ball much faster, and, although its smoother face prevented accurate and precise placing, that it would impart cut quite as severe as those of the former type. This led to a revolution in tennis; whether it led to an improvement or not may be questioned, but in tennis, as in other things, '*vestigia nulla retrorsum*'. If a golf club were invented that would drive a ball a quarter of a mile, the inventor would realise a fortune. If a new system of choke boring enabled the sportsman to kill birds at 100 yards, our breechloaders would find their way to the lumber room; but it may be doubted if golf or sport would be improved. Naturally, however, all players adopted the new method of stringing, and, in 1867, when the best play was seen in the court at Lord's, even those who were most inclined '*stare super antiquas vias*' had been constrained to accommodate their style of play to the modern implements.

The Ball

The ball used in the French *jeux* was formerly known by the name *esteuf* (even the silver ball, or blue riband of the game, was called *l'esteuf d'argent*), probably because they were made of *estouffes* or *estoupes*, de laine (Lat. *stupa*), (Gr. στυππειον στυππη).

Adulteration was not unknown in those days. M. Fourniera writes,

Les paumiers-raquettiers, qui trouvaient la laine un peu chère, mettaient dans les balles tout ce qu'ils trouvaient, surtout du son [bran]. Une ordonnance royale (Louis XI) leur rappela les devoirs du métier. Elle leur enjoignit de ne mettre en vente que des éteufs couverts de bon cuir et remplis de bonne bourre (cow's hair).

That tennis balls were stuffed with hair in England in the sixteenth and seventeenth centuries is shown by Mr Marshall, who quotes from *A Wonderful, Strange, and Miraculous Astrological Prognostication for the Year of our Lord 1591*, written by Nashe: 'They may sell their haire by the pound to stuffe tennice-balls'. Again, in *Ram Alley, or Merry Tricks, 1611*: 'Thy beard shall serve to stuff those balls by which I get me heat at tennice'. Towards the end of the seventeenth century, cotton appears to have been used in the composition of balls, for we read in Shadwell's *True Widow*, 1679, Act II, Prig: 'Methinks that old song is very pretty. My mistress is a tennis ball/Composed of cotton fine'.

These balls were covered with sheep skin or some sort of leather. In Spain, where the courts were white, black balls were used; in this country, and in France, where the tripots were always coloured black, the balls were white.

In the course of the next 100 years, ball making appears to have undergone a radical change. Hair, cotton and leather were superseded by strips of woollen material rolled tightly into a spherical form, tied with string, and covered with white cloth, and the result was a ball rather smaller, rather lighter, and less carefully finished; but in other respects similar to those we now use. Indeed, balls made as described by De Garsault in 1767, if fairly used, kept in a dry place, and recovered from time to time, are almost perennial; balls are in use now in Paris that are said to have been made seventy years ago, and which may be expected to last some years more.

The best tennis balls that are used in England are supplied by A. Tompkins & Co., No. 68 Upper Lewes Road, Brighton. These are made entirely of woollen material, and are covered with white Melton cloth, which is made expressly for the purpose at Leeds. The weight of one of these balls is 2½ oz., the diameter 2³⁄₁₆ in. It is hardly necessary to urge the importance of maintaining one standard of size, weight and elasticity, but a cloth of a finer and closer texture may be used for the covering of balls to be played with in a slow court, while for those to be used in a fast court, a softer material may be selected.

It is to be regretted that the Americans, who have recently taken up tennis with characteristic enterprise and spirit, should have failed to recognise the importance of accepting a standard that has stood the test of 100 years, and which now gives satisfaction to all experts. The balls first made at Boston were small, light and composed entirely of cotton; but as these are no longer used, they apparently failed to give satisfaction. The American balls are now of the same size and approximately of the same weight as the English balls, but, being made of alternate layers of cloth and cotton, are much slower, as the result of the following experiments demonstrates. When dropped on to the floor from the lower edge of the penthouse, a height of 7 ft 2 in., the English ball bounds to a height of 2 ft 6 in.; an English ball, at least twenty years old, 2 ft 3 in.; the American ball, 2 ft 2½ in.. Taking 1 as the coefficient of elasticity of the English ball, that of the ball of former days is -9, and that of the American ball, -88; an appreciable difference, which necessarily affects the flight of the ball after it touches the walls or floor.

If this slow ball was adopted with a view of checking the tendency to fast play, and bringing modern tennis more in harmony with the traditions of past ages, the intention is to be commended; but the durability and trustworthiness of the ball are liable to be endangered by the want of homogeneity in the material used, and the absence of a pivot that alone can give stability to the centre of gravity. In any case, the step is a retrogressive one, which will not readily find favour with young players.

3
Modern Tennis

We may not wish to encourage our wives and daughters to emulate Nausicaa, Margot, Mademoiselle Bunel, or Madame Masson, and to compete with us in an exercise fatiguing to all, and to them possibly dangerous, but we accord to them a hearty welcome when they honour the four dedans with their presence. Some ladies, indeed, have shown that the difficulty of understanding tennis is not insuperable; some are thoroughly appreciative of a good stroke, and keenly enjoy a well-contested match. But the following are examples of some strange solecisms I have heard. A lady once asked me what was kept in the yellow cupboard in the opposite corner of the court. Another asked, 'What are discs, and how do you take them?', tempting me to reply '*cum grano*', or 'two at bedtime'. Another lady, who for the first time visited the dedans at Lord's, after watching the play for some time, naively remarked to her companion, 'Why, they mark at this game just as they do at tennis!'

Nor is this want of familiarity with the game confined to our 'sisters and our cousins'. In the presence of a circle of gentlemen, some of whom were acquaintances and others strangers to me, the question was put to me, 'For how many years were you amateur champion?' I replied, 'The date could not be accurately fixed, but that I was generally credited with the enjoyment of that honour for twenty-three years'. Bewilderment and incredulity caused each particular hair on the head of one of the company to stand on end, and he was evidently saying to himself, 'Renshaw I know, and Lawford I know, but who is this?' For the moment he appeared to be doubting if he were dreaming, or if I were an impostor of more than ordinary assurance, but at last, in tones of quiet remonstrance, he said, 'I did not know that the game had been invented so long as that'.

Hoping that a perusal of these pages may prevent a repetition of such misconceptions as these, I will here offer a description of a modern tennis court, and a fuller interpretation of the terms used in the game than can be given in the appendix.

Image 11 on p. 105 represents the interior of the tennis court at the Queen's Club, West Kensington, as seen from the hazard side. The numbers indicate the component parts of the court on the service side:

1	End penthouse	8	Play line
2	Side penthouse.	9	Dedans
3	End wall	10	Last gallery
4	Main wall	11	Second gallery
5	Side wall	12	Door
6	Battery	13	First gallery
7	Gallery for spectators	14	Line opening
		15	Half court line

That part of the court that is enclosed by the main wall, the end wall, the half court line, and the net is called the forehand court; the remainder of the court on the service side is called the back hand court.

Image 12 on p. 106 represents the interior of the same court as seen from the service side; the numbers indicate the component parts of the hazard side.

1	End penthouse	9	Grille
2	Side penthouse	10	Last gallery
3	End wall	11	Second gallery
4	Main wall	12	Door
5	Battery	13	First gallery
6	Side wall	14	Line opening
7	Tambour	15	Half court line
8	Play line		

That part of the court that is enclosed by the battery, the end wall, the half court line, and the net is called the forehand court. The remainder of the court on the hazard side is called the back hand court.

Attention must next be called to the floor, on which are painted certain lines.

The half court line is drawn parallel with the side walls, dividing the court lengthways into two equal parts (except where the projection of the tambour reduces the area of the hazard side). It is used only when the odds of 'half court' are given.

The service line is drawn parallel with the end wall on the hazard side at a distance of 21 feet from it.

The pass line is drawn from the service line to the end wall, parallel with the half court line at a distance of 7 feet from it.

The area enclosed by the service line, the pass line, the end wall, and the side wall is called the service court. The area enclosed by the pass line, the service line, the end wall, and the main wall is called the pass court.

The chase lines are drawn parallel with the end walls. On the service side the line nearest to the end wall is half a yard from it, the second a yard, the third a yard and a half, the fourth two yards, and so on up to six yards. These lines indicate the 'chases', half-a-yard, a yard, 1 and 2, 2, 2 and 3, 3, 3 and 4, 4, 4 and 5, 5, 5 and 6, 6. The chase line, 'half a yard worse than 6', divides the distance between 6 and the next line, 'last gallery', which indicates a chase equivalent to that opening. The next line is 'a yard worse than the last gallery', and lines are drawn indicating chases, 'second gallery', the 'door', and the 'first gallery', and also lines midway between these lines, which show whether a chase is 'worse than a yard worse' or better than the 'second gallery', and so on. On the hazard side there are no chase lines in the service court, the first line is half a yard from the service line, the second a yard, the third a yard and a half, the fourth two yards, and there are lines that mark chases equivalent to the openings, 'second gallery', the 'door', and the 'first gallery', are also lines midway between these lines.

The chases indicated by these lines are called 'hazard side half a yard', 'hazard side a yard', and so on.

The Chase – An expression that is, to the uninitiated, what the 'Rule in Shelley's case' is to the law student, may be thus explained. When the server mistrusts his ability to return the first or any subsequent stroke of a 'rest', or when he perceives that the ball will 'fall' far before it reaches the end wall, or will return far from it, making in either case what is called a 'long chase', he makes no effort to return it; the marker observed where the ball 'falls' and calls a chase at the spot where it has 'fallen': e.g. if the ball falls on the 2 line, he calls 'chase 2'; if it 'falls' in the interval between '1 and 2' and 2, he calls 'better than 2'; if in the interval between 2 and '2 and 3', he calls 'worse than 2', and so on. No stroke is scored, but the opponents 'change sides', and 'play for the chase'. The player who made the chase – now the 'server' – tries to 'defend' it; his antagonist, now the 'striker out', tries to win it. A chase is won if the ball enters the dedans, or if it 'falls' nearer to the end wall than the ball that made the chase fell; it is lost if the ball 'falls' further from the end wall than the ball that made the chase fell. When this principle is fully grasped, the rules that apply to 'gallery chases', 'hazard side chases', and 'chase off', which are given in laws 17–23, will present no difficulty.

The Cut – As the winner of a chase scores one stroke (or 15), it is sufficiently obvious that the key to success at tennis is to make 'short chases', i.e. to play the ball so that it shall 'fall' as near as possible to the end wall. This object can best be attained by cutting the ball, or striking it with a racket held at an angle of about 45° with the floor.

A ball so struck will rotate on its vertical axis until it 'drops', will have a slight tendency to rise abruptly after it has 'dropped', and when it reaches the end wall, will 'fall' with great rapidity and apparent inelasticity. This stroke is the essence of pure tennis; for the ball, if well 'cut', may be played so that it shall drop close to the end wall, and still make a 'close chase', presenting no opportunity for return except by strokes that will presently be explained – the 'volley', the 'half volley', or the 'coup de temps'.

Twist – Horizontal spin may also be imparted to the ball (with or without cut); producing 'under hand' or 'over hand' twist. The former of these is caused when the racket is held obliquely with regard to its vertical as well as its horizontal position, and the head is moved from right to left when the stroke is made. A ball so struck will rotate on its horizontal axis from left to right. Conversely, to produce 'overhand' twist, which will cause the ball to spin from right to left, the head of the racket, which should be above the wrist of the striker, must be moved from right to left. This stroke is a valuable auxiliary to a player who is giving 'touch no walls', or 'side walls', but a tendency to twist habitually is a sure indication of a wrong position or a faulty style of holding the racket, and should be discouraged.

The Service – The spin produced by 'cut' or 'twist', or the two combined, gives infinite variety to the service, but all these countless variations emanate from the three typical openings: the 'side wall service', the 'underhand twist', and the 'drop'. To deliver the side wall service effectually, the server should stand near to the main wall at about the '4 line', and play the ball so that it shall first strike the side wall above the hazard side last gallery, then strike the penthouse, and drop in the service court near to the end wall. 'Cut' applied to the ball will cause it to 'fall' on to the floor with great rapidity; overhand twist, which will cause the ball to cling to the end wall and force the striker out into the pass court, is valuable; but underhand twist, which will have a tendency to make the ball return towards the middle of the court, will neutralise its efficacy.

The underhand twist service is given with the object of getting a 'nick'. The server should stand near to the side penthouse, at about the '3 line', and play the ball so that it shall strike the penthouse once only and 'drop' thence into the service court. If it drops in the junction of the wall with the floor, an unreturnable 'dead nick' is the result; if it strikes the end wall a few inches above the floor, it makes a 'half nick', which can best be met by a 'boast' against the side wall into the forehand court on the service side; if it drops on the floor before it reaches the end wall, it will return towards the side wall, to which it will cling closely or may even fall in the last gallery. But a failure to attain one of these objects leaves the whole court open to attack. The facility with which left-handed players can deliver this service is perhaps the only advantage they enjoy. They can impart overhand twist, which corresponds to the underhand twist of a right-handed player, with lightning speed, and fully justify the epithets 'railroad' or *chemin de fer*, which have often been applied to this service. Image 13 on p. 106 shows Pettitt in the act of delivering this service and imparting such underhand twist as he alone can impart. The 'giraffe', a branch of the underhand twist service, is delivered from the same part of the court as the last mentioned service. If sufficient elevation is given, and the ball powerfully twisted, it will drop near to the 'pass line', and may even bound into the 'grille'. Barre in former times was, and Saunders now is, a perfect exponent of this beautiful and interesting opening of the game.

In the drop service, the ball, spinning from right to left, appears to lose all its elasticity when it strikes the penthouse, and if strong overhand twist is imparted to it, it can scarcely be returned except by a volley. The server should stand near to the main wall and deliver the service so that the ball shall drop from a high elevation on to the side penthouse, not far from its junction with the end penthouse. Few players, however, can persevere in this service throughout a match, for the subsequent rapid change of position should the ball be returned into the backhand corner, and the exertion required to 'put on twist', are a strain on the strongest muscles, but it is a valuable resource in critical junctures.

On Striking Out – The objects of the player who returns the service are either to make a 'close chase', to 'win a chase', or to 'force for the dedans'. The exigencies of the moment must determine how a chase is to be made or won, but for play on the floor 'forehand cut', which is illustrated in image 14 on p. 107, is almost, if not quite, a *sine qua non*. The 'cut' may be emphasised by a slight turn of the wrist and a partial check of the forward movement of the racket at the moment the ball is struck, but these subtle refinements are difficult and dangerous, and should be resorted to with caution. The 'side wall' and 'drop' services have been robbed of some of their terrors by a feature of modern tennis – the volley from the penthouse into the corner of the opposite forehand court. This stroke had been seldom practised until Mr Gerald Balfour found that services that the narrow and steep penthouse of the Cambridge court made unusually difficult could be returned in this manner, and his example was speedily followed by Mr Ivo Bligh, Mr A. Lyttelton, and other Cambridge players. Image

15 on p. 107 illustrates the position of Saunders when making this beautiful stroke, of which he is the best living exponent.

The force is the usual resource of a player who must try to win at very 'close chase', or who returns a ball that comes 'fair off' from the end wall. Cut impedes rather than aids the speed of the 'direct force', which should be driven with a full swing of the arm, every muscle of every part of the body being brought into action; but twist materially enhances the difficulty of a successful 'stop' and 'cut', or overhand twist, will make a 'boasted force' more formidable than ever. It is impossible to force as severely, difficult to force as accurately, with a backhand as with a forehand stroke, but the intention of the player is more easily masked, and the ball arriving unexpectedly, if less swiftly, often baffles the most experienced volleyer. Image 16 on p. 108 shows the position of a player about to force for the dedans or grille.

On Return – The ball may be 'returned' forehand or backhand in its bound (or at the 'long hop'), by the 'volley', the 'half volley', or the 'coup de temps'. A player should, by a timely advance or retreat, try to avail himself of the first of these methods, as he will thus be enabled to force, or to place, or to cut the ball, and so convert defence into attack. Image 17 on p. 108 shows Saunders returning a ball backhanded with cut into the forehand corner of the opposite court.

The Volley – The apparent facility of 'hitting a full pitch' has led many a young player to underrate the difficulty of this stroke, but since it is indispensable for the defence of the dedans, and frequently useful in the return of balls, which, if allowed to drop, would present difficulty, its importance cannot be overrated. The player should observe his opponent's stroke, that he may judge the speed of the ball and anticipate the twist that may have been imparted; he should grasp his racket firmly, and should avoid striking at the ball with more than necessary force.

The half volley should be the last resource of a player for, except by accident, cut is never imparted by this stroke, and accurate placing is nearly impossible. Many balls, however, can be returned in no other way, and the graceful posture assumed by the 'half volleyer', and the brilliant, if sometimes unexpected, results of this stroke, have always made it popular in the dedans, and have evoked for it hearty, if occasionally undeserved, plaudits.

The images on pages 109 and 110 illustrate the forehand and backhand half volley.

The *coup de temps* is the 'positively last' resource of a player who must return the ball or lose a stroke. A really fine player will occasionally startle spectators by the sympathy of nerve and muscle and intuitive perception that enable him to return an almost 'impossible' stroke, but such *tours de force* must be seen to be appreciated, for they cannot be described.

The tiro, who for the first time enters the dedans of a tennis court, must not be disappointed if he fails to fathom the intention of the players in each successive stroke, and to grasp every detail of the game; but it is hoped that this exegesis – and a perusal of laws 3–10, which define the 'service'; 11–13, which relate to 'return'; and 14–27, which explain the system of scoring and of marking 'chases' – will enable him to comprehend why some apparently easy balls are left alone, while superhuman efforts are made to return others that seem to be more difficult, to follow with interest the progress of a set at tennis, and to realise that the day may not be far distant when he may become conversant with the more abstruse refinements of the game.

On Giving Odds – There is no game in which disparity of skill between the players can be neutralised by the adjustment of odds so well as in tennis. Golf players may, perhaps, challenge this statement; but in that game the individual skill of one player is pitted not so much against the individual skill of the other player, as against the hazards that have been created by nature or by art. In tennis, the receipt of points, or, if necessary, of 'cramped odds' in addition to points, will invest with interest the actual game between a champion and a tiro.

A 'bisque', or a stroke that may be claimed at any time in a set by the recipient, is the smallest point of odds usually given. One or more bisques may be given or received in augmentation of, or diminution of, other odds, e.g. half fifteen and two bisques, half court for a bisque, κ.τ.λ.

A bisque, when taken, wins not only a stroke, but also a chase that has been established; its value, therefore, is considerably in excess of one stroke, and an approximate estimate of that excess may be thus made. It is generally admitted that two bisques are equivalent to half fifteen for a bisque, hence we may infer that half fifteen equals three bisques, fifteen equals six bisques and thirty equals twelve bisques. I have on more than one occasion, as an experiment, given twelve bisques to an opponent to whom I was able to give thirty, and have found that the equation, as might be expected, held good. Now, a set may be determined in six games, it may be protracted to eleven, or, in the case of an advantage set, to more than eleven games. In the first case, the recipient of half fifteen receives three strokes, in the second five or more. Ten games may be taken as an average length of a set, so the recipient of half fifteen will, on an average, receive five strokes, and the value of three bisques may be thus estimated at five strokes. It is a time-honoured maxim that a giver of odds should take a bisque to save a game and a receiver of odds should do so in order to win a game. The exceptions are rare, but some players would not hesitate to save, or secure the ninth game of set, when the score stood at four game all.

Half fifteen, or one stroke given at the beginning of the second and every subsequent alternate game of a set.

Fifteen, or one stroke at the beginning of every game of a set.

Half thirty, or one stroke at the beginning of the first game, two strokes at the beginning of the second game, and so on alternately in all subsequent games of a set.

Thirty, or two strokes at the beginning of every game of a set.

Half forty, or two strokes at the beginning of the first game, three strokes at the beginning of the second game, and so on alternately in all subsequent games of a set.

Forty, or three strokes at the beginning of every game of a set.

Round Services – See Law 31, Chap. IV. The giver should minimise the penalty by imparting some twist to the service, but he must be prepared to act on the defensive at the commencement of each rest, and will find that these odds are equivalent to about fifteen for a bisque.

Bar the Dedans, Bar the Winning Openings, Bar the Openings – The giver of the first named of these odds loses a stroke if a ball returned by him enters the 'dedans'; of the second, if the ball returned by him enters the 'dedans', the grille, or the last gallery on the hazard side; of the third, if the ball returned by him enters the dedans, the grille, or any of the galleries, or touches a gallery post.

If the competitors are of equal strength, the worth of the dedans may be half fifteen and a bisque; of the winning openings, fifteen for a bisque; of all the openings, fifteen and a bisque; but the value of these odds is by no means constant, and is much diminished if they are given in augmentation of points. A player who is strong enough to give thirty to his opponent should confine his play to the 'floor'; indeed, some players would give thirty and the dedans in preference to thirty and a bisque, thirty and the openings in preference to thirty and two bisques.

Half Court, see Law 32, Chap. IV.

Side Walls – The giver of these odds loses a stroke if a ball returned by him touches (before it has fallen) a side wall or a gallery post, or enters a gallery. He is not precluded from playing the ball on to the penthouse. The value of half court or side walls may be estimated at half thirty and a bisque.

Touch No Walls – The giver of these odds loses a stroke if a ball returned by him touches (before it has fallen) a wall or a gallery post, or enters an opening. He is not precluded from playing the ball on to the penthouse. These difficult odds, which are equivalent to nearly, if not quite, forty, require accurate judgment and a delicate manipulation of the racket to a greater extent than any other form of tennis, and are replete with interest to the giver and to the recipient.

A few words are necessary on the duties of that useful official of a tennis court, the marker. An incompetent or careless marker tests the equanimity of the most long-suffering and good-tempered player. Even a good marker is sometimes addressed in choleric words by a splenetic player who fancies himself aggrieved by an adverse decision. A first-rate marker must, therefore, be gifted with patience, decision of character, power of concentrating his attention on his work, a voice clear and audible, but not too obtrusive, and physical strength that will enable him to stand at his post for protracted periods, and in all weathers. His duties are to call 'fault' or 'pass' as occasion requires; to call the state of the game after each stroke; to mark the chases when made; to direct the players, when necessary, to change sides; and to decide all doubtful and disputed strokes. Such strokes must occur from time to time; the most capable marker may, like Lord Eldon, doubt, or the interposition of the racket or the body of a player may even interfere with his sight of the ball, and in such emergencies the duty of the marker has never been clearly defined. In some courts, he remains silent until the 'rest' is played out, when an appeal may be made to the 'dedans', or to the umpires, should any have been appointed; in others he calls 'play', 'double', 'out of court', etc., when the stroke is made. Perhaps the best system in these cases is that he should call 'play it out', and that at the end of the rest the appeal should be made either by himself or by the player against whom he has given his decision. In all recent important matches, two umpires and a referee have been appointed; this course has given general satisfaction, and is unquestionably better than the older system of collecting the votes of all spectators who have formed an opinion, and accepting their verdict as final. The marker should also be thoroughly versed in all practical duties connected with the repair of rackets and balls, he should be a competent instructor, and a player of sufficient strength to be able to hold his own with all but the strongest amateurs.

J. Pennell, best known as 'Jimmie', the marker at Lord's, is the best living exponent of unerring accuracy, both as regards scoring the game and making chases. John Tompkins at Brighton, Peter Latham and Holden at the Queen's Club, West Kensington, Harradine at Cambridge, Alfred White at the Duke of Fife's, Ted Johnson at Lord Wimborne's, are all excellent markers. The first named of these, John Tompkins, was in the meridian of his life a very strong player, and the honours won by Latham at rackets, his youth and activity, and his accurate and graceful style, may justify his friends in predicting for him a brilliant career on the tennis court.

4

The Laws of Tennis

Perhaps there is nothing that better illustrates the excellence of the common law of tennis than the fact that the statute law, as we now have it, embodies nearly all the principles of the game as played in the earliest times of which we have any record. Messer Antonio Scaino da Salò, a priest and doctor of theology, born AD 524, is the earliest author on the subject to whom reference will be made. The *Trattato della Palla* written by him in 1555, fully explains the system of scoring the game by four strokes (each stroke counting fifteen), and the terms *a due* and *vantaggio*, from which our now familiar terms 'deuce' and 'advantage' are derived. This treatise also gives a history of 'chases', their development, and the laws relating to them that then existed. In longue paume a *caccia*, from which the French *chasse* and the English 'chase' are derived, was equivalent to the mark or marking of a ball that is sent or pursued (*cacciata*), and was formerly indicated by a piquet or standard placed at the spot where the ball ceased to roll, or was stopped after it had touched the ground a second time. But in the tripots the practice of marking the 'chase' where the ball touched the floor after its first bound soon became general, a custom highly commended by Scaino, inasmuch as it encouraged players to cut (*tagliare*) the ball.

But, although interesting from an historical point of view, Scaino's records do not show the laws of the game as then played, nor does the *Ordonnance,* made in Paris in 1592, printed in 1632 by C. Hulpean, and reprinted in the Maison Académique in 1659; but we there learn that tennis, which in Scaino's time was played by the game of four strokes, was then played by the set of four games – i.e. the best of seven games. That this practice was subsequently maintained is abundantly shown in M. de Garsault's treatise, in which is also made the first mention of the last gallery on the 'hazard side' as a 'winning opening', and of the 'chase lines', fourteen in number, marked on the floor as they are at the present time. The excellent and practical essay by Barcellon, written in 1800, tells us that by this time the set was in Paris played the best of fifteen games, as is still the custom abroad, and his reflections on the game and his advice to players are as applicable to the modern school of tennis as to the earlier disciples.

The next work deserving of notice was written by R. Lukin, who gives a description of a tennis court, and of the system of scoring the sets, an illustration of the various ways in which odds may be given, and 'the rules of the game as commonly observed in the courts in London', in a treatise that is explicit, and quite in harmony with modern practice.

But, although these books may be studied with interest by anyone who wishes to trace the steps that led to the conditions of modern play, they give no consecutive statement of the rules under which a set should be played, nor do they offer more than an outline of the laws of tennis. With a view of supplying this want, the committee of the Marylebone Cricket Club instructed a sub-committee to draft a code of rules that should be observed in their court. These laws, compiled and signed by Spenser Ponsonby, J. M. Heathcote, E. Chandos Leigh, W. Hart Dyke, and C. G. Lyttelton, were adopted in 1872 by the MCC, and are in force at some clubs and some private courts. In this code, one departure only was made from the laws handed down to us by custom or tradition in this country. Previous to 1872, if a ball dropped in the court opposite to that from which it was struck, and bounded over the net, a chase was marked at the spot where it fell. In these cases, a player was required to defend a chase that he himself had made, and this occurrence, fortunately infrequent, was found to be anomalous and confusing. The MCC code ordered that all such strokes should be marked 'chase the line', and this rule now obtains in all English courts. An attempt was also made to effect a compromise between the many ways of scoring when the ball strikes the net post; but this rule is of little interest, because in all recently constructed courts the net post is set back in the marker's compartment so that it cannot be struck.

This set of rules, however, left some points still unprovided for, except by the custom of the court, and the laws of tennis were arranged in 1878 by Mr Julian Marshall and published in the *Annals of Tennis*. This code is the most recent, explicit, and complete that has been offered to the public, and alone provides for every question that could arise in an important match. By the kind permission of the author and publisher these laws are given here.

Implements and Choice of Sides

1. Balls and Rackets – The balls shall be not less than 2¼ inches, and not more than 2⅝ inches, in diameter; and shall not be less than 2½ oz. and not more than 2¾ oz. in weight.

Note: There is no restriction as to the shape or size of the rackets.

2. Choice of Sides – (a) The choice of sides at the beginning of the first set is determined by spin.

(b) In subsequent sets of a series, the players shall begin each set on the sides on which they finished the set before it.

Service

3. Delivery – The ball served must be struck with the racket, and may be delivered from any part of the service side.

4. Service – The ball served must touch the service penthouse before touching any other part of the court, except the rest of the side penthouse and the service wall; and it must drop in the service court, or on one of the lines that bound it.

5. Service, when good – The service is good (a) if the ball served touches (in its descent) any part of the service penthouse, so as to rise again from it; or (b) if the ball served strikes the service wall, and afterwards touches (in its descent) any part of the service penthouse, even though it does not rise again from it; or (c) if the ball served drops in the winning gallery.

6. Faults not returnable – A fault may not be returned.

7. Passes not returnable – A pass may not be returned, but a ball served, which has not gone across the pass line on the penthouse,

may be volleyed, although, if untouched, it might have dropped in the pass court. If a pass touches the striker out, or if a service (before it has dropped) touches him, when standing with both feet in the pass court and not having attempted to strike the ball, it is still counted as a pass.

8. Faults annulled – A pass annuls a previous fault.

9. Service and Faults annulled – If the striker out declares himself not ready for a service, and has made no attempt to return it, that service is counted for nothing, though it be a fault. It annuls a previous fault. The striker out, having been asked if he be ready, and having declared himself ready, may not refuse a second service.

10. Continuation or Service – The server continues to serve until two chases be made, or one chase when the score of either player is at forty or advantage (see Law 25); the players then change sides, the server becomes striker out, and the striker out becomes server.

Return

11. Return, when good – The return is good if the ball in play is struck with the racket so that it passes the net without touching a gallery post or anything fixed or lying in an opening on the side from which it is struck, and without going out of court.

12. Return, when not good – The return is not good, (a) if not in accordance with the terms of Law 11; or (b) if the ball be struck more than once, or be not definitely struck; or (c) if the ball in play, having passed the net, comes back and drops on the side from which it was struck, unless it should have touched a gallery post or anything fixed or lying in an opening on that side of the court that is opposed to the striker.

13. Ball, when not returnable – A ball that is no longer in play may not be returned.

Scoring

14. The Server when he wins a stroke – The server wins a stroke (except as provided in Law 9) (a) if a good service enters the winning gallery or the grille; or (b) if the striker out fails to return a good service (except when it makes a chase – see Laws 17–19); or (c) if

the striker out fails to return the ball in play (except when it makes a chase – see laws 17–19); or (d) if he himself returns the ball in play so that it enters the winning gallery or grille, or fall on or beyond the service line; or (e) if he serves or returns the ball in play so that it drops or falls upon a ball, or other object, which is on or beyond the service line; or (f) if he wins a chase (see Law 20); or (g) if the striker out loses a stroke (see Law 16).

15. The striker out, when he wins a stroke – The striker out wins a stroke (except as provided in Law 9) (a) if the server serves two consecutive faults (except as provided in Law 31b); or (b) if the server fails to return the ball in play (except when it makes a chase – see Laws 17–19); or (c) if he himself returns the ball in play so that it enters the dedans; or (d) if he wins a chase; or (e) if the server loses a stroke (see Law 16).

16. Either Player, when he loses a stroke – Either player loses a stroke, (a) if he loses a chase (see Law 21); or (b) if the ball in play (except as provided in Law 7) touches him or anything that he wears or carries (except his racket in the act of returning the ball); or (c) if he touches or strikes the ball in play with his racket more than once, or does not definitely strike it.

17. Chases, how marked – When a ball in play (on either side of the net, not being that on which the striker is standing) (a) falls on any part of the floor, except on or beyond the service line; or (b) enters any gallery except the winning gallery; or (c) touches a gallery post. It is marked as a chase; (i) at that line on the floor on which it fell; or (ii) better or worse than that line on the floor that is nearest to the point at which it fell; or (iii) at that gallery the post of which it touched (except as provided in Laws 18 and 19).

Note (a): A ball in play, which touches the net post and drops on the side opposed to the striker is marked a chase at the line on the side on which it drops.

Note (b): A ball in play that enters a gallery is marked a chase at that gallery which it enters, notwithatanding that it may have touched an adjacent gallery post without touching the floor in the interim.

Note (c): The gallery lines on the floor correspond and are equivalent to the galleries of which they bear the names.

18. A Ball dropping or falling in net, or bounding over net after dropping, how marked – When a ball in play (a) drops or falls in the net on the side opposed to the striker; or (b) drops on the floor on the side opposed to the striker, and, bounding over the net, falls on that side of it from which it was struck, whether it touches the net in its bound or not; it is marked a chase at the line on the side opposed to the striker.

19. A Ball dropping or falling upon another ball, how marked – When a ball in play drops or falls upon a ball, or other object, which is on the floor (except when it is on or beyond the service line – see Law 14e), it is marked a chase at the point at which that ball, or other object, was when the ball in play dropped or fell upon it.

20. Chases, how won – Either player wins a chase (a) if he serves or returns the ball so that it enters a winning opening; or (b) if he serves or returns the ball so that it falls better than the chase for which he played, or enters a gallery, or touches a gallery post, better than the gallery or the gallery line, at which the chase was for which he played; or (c) if he serves or returns the ball so that it drops or falls upon a ball, or other object, which is at a point on the floor better than that at which, or at the gallery corresponding to which, the chase was for which he played; or (d) if his antagonist fails to return the ball in play, except when it falls worse than the chase in question.

21. Chases, how lost – Either player loses a chase (a) if he fails to return the ball in play, except when it falls worse than the chase in question; or (b) if he returns the ball in play so that it falls worse than the chase, or enters a gallery, or touches a gallery post worse than the gallery, or the gallery line, at which the chase was for which he played; or (c) if he returns the ball in play so that it drops or falls upon a ball, or other object, which is at a point on the floor worse than that at which the chase was for which he played.

22. Chase off – When a ball in play (a) falls at a point on the floor neither better nor worse than that at which, or at the gallery corresponding to which, the chase was for the striker played; or (b) enters that gallery, or the gallery corresponding to that gallery line, or touches the post of that gallery, or falls on the gallery line corresponding to that gallery at which the chase was for which the striker played; or (c) drops or falls upon a ball, or other object, which is at a point

on the floor neither better nor worse than that at which, or at the gallery corresponding to which, the chase was for the striker played; it is marked chase off, it is not scored as a stroke won by either player, the chase is annulled, and the striker has not to play for it again.

23. Chases when played for – As soon as two chases are marked, or one chase when the score of either player is at forty or advantage (see Law 25), the players change sides; the player who made the first chase now defends it, while the other plays to win it, and so with the second chase, except when only one has been marked.

24. Chases marked in error annulled – If by an error three chases have been marked, or two chases when the score of either player is at forty or advantage (see Law 25), the last chase in each case is annulled.

25. Strokes, how scored – On either player winning his first stroke the score is called fifteen for that player; on either player winning his second stroke, the score is called thirty for that player; on either player winning his third stroke, the score is called forty for that player; and the fourth stroke won by either player is scored game for that player, except as below:

If both players have won three strokes, the score is called deuce, and the next stroke won by either player is scored advantage for that player; if the same player wins the following stroke he wins the game; if he loses the following stroke the score is again called deuce, and so on until either player wins the two strokes immediately following the score of deuce, when the game is scored for that player.

26. Games, how scored – The player who first wins six games wins a set, except as below:

If both players win five games, the score is called games-all, and the next game won by either player is scored advantage game for that player. If the same player wins the following game, he wins the set; if he loses the following game, the score is again called games-all; and so on until either player wins the two games immediately following the score of games-all, when he wins the set.

Note: Players often agree not to play advantage sets, but to decide the set by one game after arriving at the score of games-all.

27. Doubtful and disputed cases, how decided – Every chase is marked and every stroke scored by the marker, who is entitled to

consult the dedans when he is in doubt. A player who is dissatisfied with the marker's decision is entitled to appeal to the dedans. A majority of the dedans confirms or reverses the marker's decision. An appeal must be made before a recommencement of play.

Note: The dedans should not give a decision unasked on a question of marking a chase or stroke, but may, and should, correct inaccurate scoring of chases, strokes, games, or sets.

Three-handed or Four-handed Games (Sometimes called Double Games)

28. Order of play – The partners serve and strike out in alternate games, unless it shall have been previously agreed to the contrary.

Note: It is usually, but not always, agreed that the striker out may leave to his partner such services as pass him. The former laws apply to these as well as to single games, the advantages and disadvantages attaching to a single player under the former laws attaching to a pair of players.

Odds

29. Bisques and half bisques, when taken generally – (a) A bisque or a half bisque may not be taken after the service has been delivered. (b) The server may not take a bisque after a fault, but the striker out may do so.

30. Bisques and half bisques, when taken in changing sides – A player who wishes to take a bisque or a half bisque, there being a chase or two chases marked, may take it either before or after changing sides, but he may not after changing sides go back to take it.

31. Round services – (a) When the odds of round services are given, the ball served by the giver of odds must touch the grille penthouse after touching the service penthouse, and before dropping in the service court or on one of the lines that bound it. (b) Neither faults nor failure in complying with the above conditions are counted against the giver of odds, but the recipient of odds may decline to return such services as do not touch both penthouses; if, however, he attempts and fails to return any such service it is counted against him.

32. Half court – The players having agreed into which half court, on each side of the net, the giver of the odds shall play, the latter

loses a stroke if the ball, returned by him, drops in either of the other half courts; but a ball returned by the giver of odds which (a) drops on the half court line; or (b) drops in his half court, and touches the dedans post before falling; or (c) drops in his half court and falls in the dedans, even though on the other side of the dedans post; or (d) touches the dedans post before dropping; is counted for the giver of odds. A return, boasted against any wall by the giver of odds, which (e) drops in his half court; or (f) drops on the half court line; or (g) touches the dedans post before dropping; or (h) touches any penthouse , battery, or wall before dropping in his half court, dropping on the half court line or touching the dedans post; is also counted for the giver of odds.

Note: It is of course evident that the giver of these odds may make a chase, or win a chase or a stroke, with a ball that drops in his half court or on the half court line, but falls in the other half court.

33. Nicks, when all the walls or side walls are given – When the odds of touch no walls or touch no side walls are given, a ball returned by the giver of odds, which makes a nick, is counted for the striker.

I will add a few comments on the principles involved in some of these laws, pointing out where they, in the opinion of some players, still fall short of absolute perfection, and showing in what particulars they differ from the rules enforced in France.

Law 4 prohibits a service that, although forbidden by the rules given in Lukin's treatise, has been subsequently practised in several tennis courts. In Paris it is termed *le service martele* or *pique*. The ball is hammered or struck with considerable force on to the penthouse above the second or last gallery, whence it flies rapidly to the end wall near the pass line, and not unfrequently bounds into the grille. It is a mechanical stroke, easily learned and devoid of interest; it gives an undue advantage to the server, and is very properly condemned by all lovers of tennis.

Law 8 can only be defended by the plea that it has been the custom for many generations. The committee of management of the court at Machester passed a by-law in 1884 enacting that in their court a pass shall not annul a previous fault, and this simple but bold measure of reform is to be highly commended.

Law 12 (b) very properly precludes a player from catching and, as it were, throwing the ball over the net, when by an accidental rebound it has clung so close to the end wall that a definite stroke is impossible. As Barcellon pointed out ninety years ago, writing in condemnation of this practice, if a player may hold the ball even for a fraction of a second, he cannot logically be prevented from holding it for an indefinite period, and even from running up to the net still keeping the ball on the strings of his racket.

It is not easy to see how this subsection could be more explicitly worded, but a stroke was recently occurred at Brighton in actual play that illustrates the difficulty of providing legislation for every possible contingency. In this case, the striker out, having to play for a short 'chase', forced very hard and with accurate aim for the 'dedans'. The ball grazed the racket of the server, and, slightly deflected from its course, struck the 'bandeau' above the 'dedans', whence it returned over the net, without touching the floor on the service side, and dropped on to the floor on the hazard side. If the server can be said to have definitely struck the ball when he tried to stop the 'force' with a volley, the return was a good one, and fulfilled the conditions of Law 11, but nothing save a wild flight of imagination could suggest that such a stroke was definite in any sense of the word. The incident, or rather accident, is probably unique in the annals of tennis, and is mentioned here more on account of its unparalleled eccentricity than as showing the necessity for provision against its recurrence.

Law 17 (first note) is not a satisfactory solution of this question, but it is at least as good as the MCC rule, which makes the net post 'out of court', or the ancient custom of treating the post as if it were a portion of the net, and considering all balls that passed over the net to be 'in play', although they might have touched the net, the net post, or the hook that fastens the net to the main wall. The last of these is the most logical, but it is inconvenient, and it is to be hoped that the elimination of the net post from all tennis courts may render all legislation on the subject unnecessary.

Law 17 (second note) is in accord with the past and present practice of French courts, but is an innovation in this country. In Lukin's treatise on tennis the law is thus worded: 'If a ball touch the post of a gallery, or door, or the post of the "dedans", it is to be marked as if it entered such gallery, door, or "dedans"'; and this ruling remained unchallenged in England until 1878. In favour of Mr Marshall's alteration, it can be urged that a ball may enter a gallery after touching a post so lightly that the attention of the marker may not have been called to the fact of its having done so; but I would venture to submit in defence of the English custom that a ball that has touched a post is dead, and therefore no longer in play, and that it is in accordance with reason and logic that the stroke shall be marked at the spot where to all intents and purposes the 'rest' was actually determined.

Law 22 is opposed to the practice in foreign countries. Scaino and all subsequent writers bear testimony to the custom of playing for a 'chase' that has been established as often as may be necessary, until it is either won or lost. No important principle, however, is involved, and the method of disposing of 'chase off' that obtains on the Continent offers no advantages over the custom that has always prevailed in England.

Law 26 makes compulsory what formerly was optional. Thirty years ago, the set was usually determined by the eleventh game. Advantage sets were then exceptional, and were played only with the consent of both players, but the law is in accord with the general practice of modern players, and with the traditions of Continental tennis.

Other discrepancies exist between the English and foreign systems of scoring and marking, the result of the employment of a different language and a different unit of length, but our general laws are, with the few exceptions above mentioned, so nearly identical with those of other nations, that a few hours' experience will suffice for the acquisition of familiarity with the idiosyncrasies of foreign practice in any court in any country.

Long Fives

The laws of tennis are also applicable to long fives, except that in this exercise no chases are marked, and that the game is played eight or eleven up instead of by the set. Every stroke, therefore, in this form of the game must be returned, except when a ball enters a gallery (the winning gallery only excepted) or returns from the end walls beyond the service line on the hazard side, or beyond the last gallery line on the service side. Such strokes are called 'lets', and neither player is credited with the gain of a point. In this country, the player who first wins eleven strokes wins the game. Before commencing to play it is usual to 'spin' for the choice of sides, and to change sides after each subsequent game. The server has a distinct disadvantage; if the competitors are of equal strength the striker out must concede four points (in a game eleven up) to his adversary, and will still have a slight advantage.

This game is known in France by the name of *restes*, and, though not mentioned by any early writers, it is probably one of great antiquity, and we may conjecture that it was the usual exercise in the tripots before the introduction of chases.

The Unwritten Law of Tennis

Reference must also be made to the unwritten law, which can only be enforced by a spirit of courtesy, and by acquiescence in the practice of former ages.

There is an ancient custom for which little can be said, except that it is an ancient custom, that a player who has lost a love set shall pay a shilling to the marker – a cruel and wanton aggravation of the annoyance usually felt by anyone who has been so signally defeated. The refinement of this injury is carried even a step further in France: the marker on these occasions steps from his compartment into the court opposite to that occupied by the unfortunate victim, kisses the net rope, and saying, '*Bredouille, monsieur*', makes a bow expressive of his claim to the customary *douceur*.

No penalty is attached to the intentional service of a pass delivered with a view of removing a previous fault; there is no rule that prevents a player who has to defend a close chase from leaving balls lying on the floor so that his adversary's stroke may drop or fall on one of them and so lose the chase. The dangerous practice of forcing hard for the 'dedans' when the ball has returned from the end wall beyond the service line is not prohibited, but, like a premeditated 'stymie' at golf or, an intentional revoke at whist, such tactics are properly condemned by that chivalrous feeling that is instrumental in maintaining the high character of tennis.

Glossary

Balle à la main – A ball 'in play' that offers an opportunity for a decisive stroke.

Bandeau – The lintel or plate that is between the lower edge of a penthouse and an opening.

Battery – That part of the side wall that is below the galleries.

Bisque – The recipient of a 'bisque' can claim one stroke at any time in one set.

Boast, to – To return the ball so that it strikes either of the side walls before it strikes the end wall.

Chase – A stroke in abeyance, which has been made by one player, and must be played for by the other. See Laws 17–24.

Coup de temps – A return executed more by intuitive perception than by observation of the flight of the ball.

Cut – To impart vertical spin to the ball with the racket.

Dedans – The opening in the end wall on the service side of the court (the spectators present in this gallery are sometimes called the 'dedans').

Defend – A player who prevents or tries to prevent his opponent from winning a chase that he has made is said to 'defend' the chase.

Double – A ball struck after it has touched the floor a second time.

Drop – A ball is said to 'drop' when it touches the floor or the post of an opening, or enters an opening without having previously touched any part of the court, except a wall, or a penthouse, or the net.

Fair off – A ball is said to be 'fair off' when it returns from the end wall and offers an opportunity for an easy stroke.

Fall – A ball is said to 'fall', when, after having dropped, it touches the floor again, or touches the net, or enters an opening.

Fault – A service that fails to comply with the conditions of a 'good' service. See Laws 4–6.

First stroke – The return of the service.

Force – A stroke played, either direct or boasted, for the dedans with some strength. A ball tossed or played gently is not called a 'force'.

Galleries – The openings beneath the side penthouse on each side of the net.

Good – A stroke is 'good' if it is played in accordance with the provisions of the laws.

Grille – The opening in the end wall on the hazard side of the court.

Half volley – To strike the ball immediately after it has dropped.

Hazard side – That part of the court that is between the net and the end wall, on the left of the marker's compartment.

In play – A ball served or returned is said to be 'in play' until it has fallen, or has entered an opening, or has gone out of court, or has touched a gallery post, or a player, or unless it be a fault

Love game – A game in which one player wins four consecutive strokes, or, in the case of deuce and advantage, five consecutive strokes.

Love set – A set in which one player wins six consecutive games, or, in the case of an advantage set, seven consecutive games.

Nick – A stroke in which the ball dropping or falling touches the floor and wall simultaneously.

Openings – The dedans, grille, and galleries. The dedans, grille, and the last gallery on the hazard side are called the winning openings.

Pass – A service that, not being a fault, drops in the court between the passline and the main wall, or goes across the pass line on the penthouse.

Rest – A 'rest' commences when the service is delivered, and continues so long as the ball is in play.

Return – To play the service or any subsequent stroke of a rest back over the net.

Service – The starting of the ball in play. See Laws 3–10.

Service side – That part of the court that is between the net and the end wall on the right of the marker's compartment.

Stop – To prevent (by a volley) a ball from entering an opening.

Strike out – To receive the service, and so to play the first stroke.

Twist – To impart horizontal spin to the ball with the racket.

Volley – To strike the ball in play before it drops.

5

Hints to Beginners

The relation of any one particular game to other games has been but little considered, and few games present more opportunities for such consideration than tennis. With lawn tennis, indeed, the relation of tennis is literally parental, though the ordinary laws of evolution here sustain a singular reversal. In the world of nature, we are accustomed to observe the development of the rude into the highly finished, of the primitive into the complex, of the inferior into the superior. Here, however, the process is changed. The inferior has been the successor of the superior, and the offspring is cast in far more primitive form than the sire. Dedans and gallery, tambour and grille, have been lost in the struggle for existence; hazard side and chase are deemed not the fittest to survive. Advantages must be claimed, indeed, for the child not possessed by the father. A lawn, a racket, a soft ball, a net, a pot of paint, and an active member of either sex, here are all the materials needed for lawn tennis, and every country house and most suburban villas can supply them; while for tennis, the pastime of kings, such a panoply is needed that a royal income must be won to provide it.

Though no connection so close can be traced between tennis and other ball games, no one can have played cricket or rackets without finding that there is much that can be imported from those fine games into a tennis court, and much that can be taken from the tennis court back to them. Cricket may, indeed, be played contemporaneously with any of the three games above mentioned without much difficulty, though, of course, with some loss of finish; but as a rule the other three games cannot be played contemporaneously with any satisfaction. Tennis is an exacting mistress, and if a racket player wishes to woo her with success, he must seek against his former bride, not merely judicial separation, but actual decree of divorce. Some, indeed, there have been – but these are of no common clay – who on Monday have felt the tumultuous glow inspired by rackets, and on Tuesday have been able to pass unruffled by these sensuous joys to the subtler pleasures of the ancient game. But the faculty is rare, and those only who have watched Mr Ivo Bligh among gentlemen, and Pettitt and Peter Latham among professionals, will credit its existence. With this word of warning, let us hasten to say that these games frequently touch each other, and that the aptitudes for the one, by a little thought and a good deal of practice, may be transformed into finished skill in the others.

In all ball games one common law prevails. Force is imparted most effectively, not by expenditure of bodily strength only, but by the application of it to the ball at precisely the right time, and in precisely the right way. Now to time a ball depends entirely on the eye, or, in other words, on a fine observation by the player of the course taken by a ball that is hit from a particular position in a particular way, and that may have to strike against or fall on to certain objects, notably ground, floor or walls, before there is a convenient opportunity of striking it. Now this eye or fine faculty of observation can never be taught. Practice improves it, but the strange fact remains that men of high intelligence (and not short-sighted) continue for years to witness the ordinary flight of an ordinarily struck ball, and habitually run to the place where it is not going instead of to the place where the experience of 1,000 strokes ought to prove that it must go. Months elapse before the simple phenomenon presented by a ball falling on the floor, bounding against the wall, and coming off again, is tolerably apprehended. Most ladies believe that a ball struck horizontally over a net will bound off the ground vertically as if it had been dropped straight from the skies. Another aspect of the same fact can be observed in shooting. Many statesmen and almost all lawyers shoot not in front of but straight at a bird flying across or over them. Unquestionably these errors are illustrations of what, but for the eminence of the offenders, one would call a form of stupidity. But they are almost ineradicable. A good eye, in a word, is born and is not made. As, therefore, to time a ball depends chiefly on eye, 'timing' can hardly be taught. 'I see the ball, and I hit it,' Dr W. G. Grace said when asked how he managed to 'time' so finely. This answer recalls the reply of the boatswain to the noble owner of a yacht. 'Why is it,' said the owner, 'that you call the spar at the bottom of that sail the jib-boom?'

'My lord, whatever else could you call it?' Dr Grace and the boatswain disappointed their questioners, but in both cases it would puzzle anyone to give a better explanation.

Far otherwise, however, is it with regard to the second rule of skilful application of force, viz. to hit the ball in the right way. Anyone, if he is patient and docile, can be taught position, and if he is fairly well made, and has not rowed or drilled or ridden too much, can get his legs and arms to swing freely.

But the matter that is brought home most forcibly to anyone who has played the four games under consideration is that the position of the legs is of the most vital moment in the creation of a good style. The most valuable hint I ever received at any game was from E. Johnson, formerly one of the markers at Lord's tennis court. In common with most tennis players, at the outset of my experience in that game I had found great difficulties in acquiring a satisfactory return. Johnson had often watched the cricket at Lord's and had observed forward play in that game. He had the wit to see that the position of the batsman's left leg was all important, and that according as the impact of the bat on the ball was simultaneous with the descent of the left leg on the ground so the forward stroke tended to be powerful and clean. In other words, he had seen that the secret of forward play is not to advance the left leg first and then play forward with the arms and wrists, but to make the two motions simultaneously. The reason is simple and is easily explained. Such a method adds the weight of the body to the swing of the arms and the strength of the wrist. Johnson held the opinion, and he was perfectly correct, that this method should be imported into the tennis court, and that when the heavy tennis ball was struck at the player, he should meet it not merely with wrist and arm, but with weight of body applied by advancing the leg as in forward play at cricket. I found this opinion to be absolutely well founded, and in a few days the adoption of the principle revolutionised my play. The return of a ball played strongly into the forehand court at tennis is achieved by forward play differing only from the forward play of a cricketer by the stroke being performed by one hand instead of two, and by a racket moved horizontally instead of a bat moved vertically. So much for the forehand tennis return; but the backhand return receives even greater assistance from an observation of the forward play of a left-handed batsman. The right leg of such a batsman performs precisely the same functions in forward play as that of the left leg of the right-handed batsman. Figure the left-handed batsman now playing forward with his right hand only holding the bat. Here you have exactly the correct position of the backhand stroke of a right-handed man at rackets. Make the line of the arm horizontal instead of vertical, and you have the exact position of the tennis backhand stroke. Here is an opportunity for the most happy application of the painfully acquired aptitudes of one game to the needs of another. I have found very few difficulties connected with 'return' play – none, indeed, save those resulting from infirmity of eye – that are not solved by this method, which may safely be commended to all cricketers who are also players of tennis and rackets. The reason for setting so much store on the position of the legs is that the legs, far more than the arms, convey, concentrate, and apply the weight of the body to the ball about to be struck.

Many beginners keep their legs close together when they hit a ball at tennis or rackets, with the result that the whole force has to be gathered from the swing of the arm and the power of the wrist. A strong and flexible man can hit a ball hard even in such a manner, but he will hit it ten times as hard if he so adjusts and disposes his legs as to bring to the aid of his arms all the weight of his body. These considerations are of importance in cricket, tennis, rackets, and lawn tennis, though they are less important in the last two games than in the first, and for this reason: the ball used in rackets and lawn tennis is a light one, and so is the racket; thus the wrist and arm are more competent to deal with it unaided than with the heavy implements used in cricket and tennis. The ball games under consideration occupy a middle position between games such as billiards, where the arm and wrist and fingers do the whole work, and rowing, where, we are told, the arms should be simply ministerial – mere connecting – rods to apply the weight of the body to the oar.

At cricket and tennis, and rackets in particular, as has been shown, the legs and body play important parts, but there are still many fine strokes in which wrist and arm are alone concerned. I may give as instances, in cricket, 'back play', performed almost entirely by the wrist of the lowest hand on the bat, and the light underhand 'chuck' or throw in from cover point; in tennis, the 'stop' of a force at full length of arm; in rackets, the picking up of a ball almost behind the player by a turn of the wrist.

Certain it is, then, that these games have close connection, for it has been shown that the principles that ought to regulate the disposition of force apply in all of them; that, e.g. forward play in cricket exhibits features that should be copied into the other games whenever it is a question in them of striking with force and firmness a ball well pitched up. But there are, in addition to this main point, many other features of affinity. The ordinary hard forehand stroke at rackets is literally reproduced in the straight force of tennis; substitute bat for racket, add the left hand, and pitch the ball up a little farther, and you will find that a racket or tennis player will soon be a proficient in the straight drive of cricket. In general, a good service at rackets will help to that end at tennis, while a tennis player by his service in a racket court will, for a time, baffle the most skilful opponent.

But while there are these fundamental affinities between these games, there are, of course, very great differences. It is not proposed to enter into the details of these differences; they are sufficiently obvious to need no minute description here, where it is hoped rather to treat of things a little below the surface. Some few observations may, however, perhaps be offered by way of assistance to those who are passing or intending to pass from one game to another, in order to obviate, or if not to obviate at least to explain, their difficulties in the process.

Take first the case of a tennis player who wishes to amuse himself when it is too hot to play tennis by an excursion upon the lawn. At first, no doubt, he will find that every stroke that he deems good will go about 6 inches out of court, but when he has overcome that preliminary difficulty he is met by one more fundamental. If a good game between good lawn tennis players be carefully watched, it becomes apparent that the finish of nearly every good rally will be accomplished by the strong overhand volley or 'smash', or else by a 'placed' ball falling just inside the side line and passing just out of the reach of the player, who is standing in the middle of the court. It is soon manifest, therefore, that though accuracy is a necessity, accuracy alone will be of no avail in first-class company unless it is accompanied by rapidity of stroke. By rapidity of stroke is meant a method that will cause the flight of the ball to be quick through the air and far bounding when it hits the ground. Now the tennis player will soon attain accuracy both of strength and also of placing, but unless he abandons his nature he will be unable to get rapidity of stroke as above defined. His heavily cut ball will have a curved and not a very rapid flight through the air. No doubt, if it is permitted to get to the ground, the ball thus cut will come very quickly off it, but by reason of the comparatively slow flight a good player will always be able to volley it. A lawn tennis player achieves this rapidity of stoke by playing with the full face of the racket and by not attempting to cut the ball at all. If the tennis player is to attain such a stroke, he must abandon that which gives him eminence at tennis, and he must hit the ball in a manner that, if pursued within four walls, will reduce him to the fourth rank of performers. Probably he will be unable to do this even if he were willing to try, for the task will be almost analogous to bowling with another man's action.

In somewhat less degree these observations apply, *mutatis mutandis*, ti the change from tennis to rackets. The difficulties of adapting a roundhand to an underhand stroke, of modifying 'cut' into twist, of transforming the quiet curved flight of the heavy into the strong, direct course of the light ball are obvious; but they are not so insuperable as those above averted to, for rackets and tennis are unlike lawn tennis, inasmuch as they permit great force to be applied to the ball, whereas one of the great difficulties of lawn tennis is that, while it imposes enormous strain on the legs and lungs of the player, it demands from him simultaneously a softness and restraint of play such as it is most difficult to exhibit under such strenuous circumstances. My experience is that a little tennis will improve a good racket player. It will add cut to his service, it will fortify his return from the backhand corner, and it will tend to make him long-headed. On the other hand, if rackets are once and for all abandoned after tennis is taken up, the training they have given will never be regretted. This training will have unloosed the joints of the shoulder and strengthened the sinews of the wrist. It will have given a good notion of the manner in which a ball will come off a wall; it will impress the necessity of a close observation, not merely of the ball itself, but of the manner in which the ball has been hit by your opponent; it will enable you to send the ball into the dedans in a manner which will defy the surest of 'stops'.

A good cricketer, if he gives time to them, will probably be able to play at any of the games in question. Such a one must have a good eye, a good wrist and good judgment. If he can appreciate the course a ball will take off so changing a surface as that of the ground exposed to all weathers, he will have little difficulty in shrewdly guessing where it will go after being hit by a racket at lawn tennis or rackets when he has only to deal with the most carefully preserved lawns and the smoothest walls and floors. If indeed he is harassed by the numberless curves that are imparted to a tennis ball's hairy surface by the strong heavy racket, the situation will not be wholly strange to one who has dealt with a really good bowler vaunting himself on a crusty wicket. As rowing generates inaptitude for the ball games here discussed, cricket gives aptitudes to all such games, while at the same time it is not so like them as injuriously to affect the style of one who passes from the wickets to the courts. Herein lies the difficulty of dealing with the other three games. They are sufficiently like each other to make it very difficult to pass from one to the other without carrying to some extent the methods of one into the practice of the other. A lawyer when he goes into Parliament is far more at home than an untrained speaker, but if he continues to frequent the forum, he will never probably strike quite the true not for the senate. The two places are like and yet unlike. Just so a lawn tennis player will come into a tennis court. For a time he will far surpass those who have not had his training, but if he still performs on the lawn, his stroke at tennis will lack that sacred fire that a rival who is not a lawn tennis player without his initial facility may ultimately attain.

It may be observed in conclusion that cricket, rackets, lawn tennis, and even tennis itself, when once the court is built, are well within the reach of moderate incomes, make small encroachments on a man's time, and can be enjoyed and sufficiently practiced by very hard-worked men of sound constitution. As a proof of this, a very eminent member of the present cabinet joins the best amateurs either in tennis or lawn tennis and still makes strokes that will arouse their envy and despair. Some say that a fine scholar need fear no branch of learning, and that a senior classic can turn his brains to any subject. With more truth it maybe affirmed that a good cricketer has an eye and hand trained to anything, and that he is halfway to being proficient in three other excellent games. The like cannot be said of some splendid exercises. Riding to hounds, the finest of outdoor pursuits, will not help you in any other game or sport except polo. A first-rate shot has to learn every other amusement from the very beginning. Rowing, the best of bodily trainings, positively unfits a man for games, and, unless your way in the world leads you to the banks of a river, can rarely be pursued after academic life is closed.

Let all therefore learn cricket who wish to have the power in the midst of mental toil to banish every good thought of work, for cricket lies at the root of most good games, and youth without good games is gloomier than age without whist.

Two important lessons may be learned by a perusal of these pages: that correct style can only be acquired by the man who, either by precept or practice, has learned to adopt the right position of body when he makes his stroke, and that force can only be properly applied to the ball by one whose hand and eye are in sympathy.

I will try with some further illustrations of these and other attributed that are indispensable to the tennis player to assist the tiro to answer a question I have often put to myself, and which others have often put to themselves before now: 'How can I put half fifteen on to my game?'

In order to become proficient in so difficult a game as tennis, it is necessary that a player should be possessed not only of what is commonly called a 'good eye' and the physical advantages of some strength and activity, but also of the mental attributes of patience and perseverance, and that quality that is better expressed by the old Roman word *virtus* than by any equivalent in our language. To any man thus gifted by nature, who can being to learn the game when first '*tondenti barba cadit*', who has opportunity for frequent practice, and who will condescend to take advice from those who are competent to give it, will surely come those essential qualifications, accurate judgement and correct style. Now when I talk of correct style, I do not mean that there is but one correct style. The service, the first stroke and the return admit of infinite variety. Barre, 'Biboche', Edmund Tompkins, George Lambert, Pettitt, Saunders, M. Mosneron, Mr C. G. Taylor and Mr Lyttelton have had little in common except a high standard of excellence, and it would be as ideal to compare the methods employed by these players as to contract Velasquez with Sir F. Leighton, Claude Lorrain with J. C. Hook, or David Cox with Vicat Cole. But I would ask the tiro to remember that much may be learned by careful observation of the strategy of any really good player, by noticing at what crisis of the game a bisque should be taken, what kind of service is the most effective when chases, long or close, must be defended, and how the opportunities for playing for the openings or making use of the boast may be resorted to.

Misconceptions have frequently arisen on the question of eye. So many short-sighted persons have, with the aid of glasses, succeeded in becoming good players, that even organic imperfection does not seem to be an insuperable obstacle to success; moreover, I believe that if the eyes of Pettitt or John Roberts were submitted for examination to an oculist, they would not necessarily be found to differ materially from the eyes of men who have failed conspicuously at tennis or billiards. I believe rather that most of us are supplied by Providence with retina, pupil, and humours – the component parts of that beautiful engine, the human eye – in a perfect state, but that some persons, even in early childhood, display that magical sympathy between hand and eye that enables them to control the bat, the racket, or the cue almost by instinct. This sympathy must be felt to be understood, but it may be illustrated by the consciousness of its absence in a man who feels that he is off his shooting. More shots are missed by a too early or too late pressure of the trigger, or, in other words, by a want of sympathy between hand and eye, than from any other cause. So, when we remember that in order to play a tennis ball as it should be played, it must be struck at exactly the right moment with the centre of the racket, which must meet the ball at the right angle or inclination, and that, if all these conditions are not fulfilled, the ball will be lifted, twisted, or missed altogether, we may well realise how indispensable is this sympathetic action of nerve and muscle. I made use of the word some strength and activity advisedly, because I do not think that he 'Whose standing muscles slope/As slopes a wild brook o'er a little stone', has any great advantage over a less powerful opponent, and although some agility is required in reaching far off balls, I believe that it was truly said 'a good player can generally get to the ball, and that to a first-rate player the ball always comes'. I believe that, fortunately for him, 'cujus ætas undecimum trepidavit claudere lustrum' (if I may be permitted to turn Horace's well-known sapphic into a hexameter), the difficulty of masking the stroke and playing the ball away from an adversary is so great that it is generally possible to anticipate the intention of an opponent, and to arrive in time to return the ball with an effort more or less great.

Perhaps the only imperfection in the game of tennis is that it lacks the *esprit de corps* so noticeable in cricket, football and other games in which members of a team are mutually dependent on each other, and when the success of one is the success of all. But this very imperfection is one that imperatively demands from a player confidence in his own powers and courage in playing an uphill game. That there is but little luck in tennis may be inferred from the fact that a bisque, taken or received, will materially alter the chances of success, while the odds of half fifteen, or approximately one stroke in eight, would make the issue of a match between two equal players nearly a certainty. Nevertheless, occasional 'flukes' will occur; a ball played on to the penthouse that might have been expected to afford opportunities for a crushing stroke will sometimes bound into the dedans or cling so close to the end wall as to be almost unreturnable; balls will now and then glance from the bandeau or bound from the upper part of the tambour into the winning gallery. Accidental nicks will occur, and chance, success, or whatever we like to call it, will sometimes favour one competitor, while his opponent is missing his hazards by half inches. These reverses must be encountered with pluck and patience and that spirit that prevents a man from knowing when he is beaten. But this confidence must be restrained within reasonable limits, for nothing is a greater source of annoyance to spectators, nothing tends more to alienate their sympathy, than conceit; nothing is more prejudicial to improvement than unwillingness to receive the proper odds from a superior player. Something may also be learned by a study of theoretical principles, which may be observed in this as in almost every game of skill, but it is useless to rely too much on that philosophy that will 'clip an angel's wings, and conquer all mysteries by rule and line'. There is no rule and line at tennis, but philosophy, if it cannot teach us execution, can show us how to avoid faults. At cricket we are told to play with a straight bat, in rowing to catch the beginning, but experience has always shown, and will always show, how little theory will do for us without constant practice.

The surest key, therefore, to success is practice, assiduous practice, aided by ambition and encouraged by the elation consequent on well-earned victory. So the tiro is recommended always to play to win, always to exert himself as if a kingdom were at stake, and to avoid that careless and desultory style of play that may have often been observed in former years, but which is of less frequent occurrence among modern athletes. Over and over again has a set been snatched from the fire by the resolute and patient player from an over confident antagonist, who, thinking that he had the game in his hands, served carelessly or took balls that ought to have been left, and left balls that ought to have been taken. When he has once 'dropped his game', the careless player will find it hard to resume his former precision, and will discover too late that, in spite of strenuous efforts, the set, and perhaps the match, may be irretrievably lost.

But one essential requirement remains to be mentioned; an income sufficient to provide for the devotion of from 25*l* to 30*l* to this amusement, and here I would endeavour to remove the misconceptions that prevail touching the excessive cost of the game of tennis. Should a wandering player enter a court in the neighbourhood where he may happen to be staying, and play for a casual hour or two with the marker, he may not find the amusement commensurate with the expense; but if he becomes an annual subscriber at one of the many courts where privileges are accorded to the regular players, or is a member of one of the clubs to which a tennis court is attached, he will find that the cost of play will be about 2s per hour only (in some courts the charge is rather more, in some it is less), and 10l a year will defray the subscription and the amount necessary for the purchase and repair of rackets. The charge for the game of rackets, including the price of balls, will amount to quite as much, and an enthusiastic pursuit of billiards will absorb more time and as much money.

Football, boating, golf, and lawn tennis are, no doubt, cheaper amusements; but I believe that the devotees of hunting, shooting, or cricket know that their recreation costs an amount in excess of that which I have named, during the brief season in which they can pursue their avocations, while tennis players are privileged to indulge in their pastime at any season of the year, and in any weather.

This calculation is based on the assumption that an amateur is able to devote to the game four hours in the course of a week during six months of the year. Only a favoured few can spare more time than this; but it will be found that, although accuracy of execution and judgment may be subsequently matured, five or six years of such practice will enable any amateur to attain to nearly the highest standard of play to which he may aspire.

A few practical suggestions, based on the experience of many years, may be of service to the tiro at the outset of his career, and, as he must provide himself with the necessary implements, I will first call his attention, to the selection of a racket. He should choose a hoop free from knots, or any imperfection in the grain of the wood, and should reject any that appear to be top heavy, for he must remember that the gut with which the racket will be strung will add nearly an ounce and a half to the weight of the hoop. The 'fulcrum' of a well-balanced racket will be at a point in the handle about ¼ inch from the screw. This can be tested with sufficient accuracy before selection is made. I never select a racket for my own use of less weight than 423, or more than 427 grams, but perhaps I am unnecessarily exigent in this matter; one whose weight is between 420 and 430 grams will be found to be suitable to most players. Lighter rackets have not sufficient game in them, and are liable to be broken, while those that are heavier are less manageable except by very strong men. The weight of rackets is marked, usually on the end of the handle, before they are imported into this country, and the accuracy of the figures may be relied on with confidence.

The question will be asked by the beginner, 'How am I to hold my racket?' I answer, 'In the most easy and natural way possible, bearing in mind only that its normal position when a stroke is made should be at an angle of about 45° with the floor. The handle should be grasped as lightly as is consistent with immunity from danger of its turning in the hand when the ball is struck, the thumb and forefinger being in contact, resting on the left side near its upper edge, the other three fingers being brought round, so that their tips shall rest on its upper side. The racket should not be held too long, i.e. grasped at a point too near the end of the handle, nor too short, i.e. too near the middle piece, for if it is held too long, inaccuracies of judgment will be emphasised, while if it is held too short, reach and severity must be sacrificed, and an unskilful player may inflict a blow on his own chest or knee should the ball make an unexpected bound. Believing that a long leverage would to some extent compensate for a want of muscular power, I taught myself to play with a long racket, but I seldom play two consecutive strokes without changing my grasp, and the young player will do well to accept no dogma, but to find out for himself how he can best continue severity with accuracy.

When he enters the court let him resolve never intentionally to violate the three canons of tennis:

1. To face the side wall, not his adversary.
2. To strike the ball in its descent.
3. To support the head of the racket, or, in other words, to keep the hoop at as high an elevation as is compatible with freedom.

Of these the first is the most important; indeed, until a player has adopted it as his second nature he can scarcely hope to play the ball with a backhand stroke over the net. It scarcely needs demonstration that vertical spin or 'cut' will be more easily imparted to a falling than a rising ball, when it meets with the oblique face of a racket, and that although an upright racket may impart horizontal spin or twist to the ball, it will not cause the vertical spin that produces cut. He must remember that when he plays the ball forehanded, the right foot must be the pivot, the other foot being left free to be moved as occasion may require, and to be brought on to the floor immediately before the execution of the stroke, and, conversely, that the left foot must be the pivot when a backhanded stroke is necessary. That these maxims have been considered important may be illustrated by an anecdote of an enthusiast who had been taking a lesson from a French *paumier* in the morning, and who, on his way from the court, was practising ideal strokes with his umbrella in the Champs Elysees. In answer to an anxious inquiry from a friend who had not been initiated into the mysteries of tennis, '*Que faites-vous là?*' he replied, '*Mais, par exemple, j'exerce mon arrière main*', and no doubt was thought a fit and proper inmate for the '*maison des aliénés*'. Nature will soon show that the knees should be slightly bent, and that the attitude should be such as will admit of rapid change of posture, but she will not suggest the conventional dogmas about bending the body that we sometimes hear, and a study of the postures of good players will show that it is just possible to 'conquer without stooping'.

For his first practice, let him stand near the last gallery on the service side of the court and play the ball against the main wall, as he would play a ball in a racket court, and return it forehanded or backhanded over and over again, until he has learnt to judge its bound and to place it with some certainty. This should be soon mastered, but he will experience greater difficulty when he commences the next practice, viz. to toss the ball up on the penthouse, let it drop on to the floor, and then play it over the net. Here the advice of a competent 'mentor' will be of inestimable value, for many beginners allow the ball to get too far in front of them, and find that they can do no more than spoon the ball with perhaps some twist, and many in their anxiety to cut the ball play with the racket too 'open', i.e. with the hoop too horizontal, scarcely allowing themselves a chance of striking the ball fairly with the strings. These faults should be pointed out and rectified before they become confirmed habits. It will also be found useful to toss a ball against the main wall and to cut it with a forehanded stroke over the net, still more useful to play a similar stroke backhanded after tossing a ball against the opposite wall; for, although this stroke cannot occur in a game, it is the easiest and simplest way of learning cut without twist. He should also practise the delivery of a service, and should observe the effect that the cut or twist he may have imparted to the ball has on its course after it touches the penthouse, walls or floor.

For his next exercise he should take a basketful of balls to the hazard side of the court, and tossing them one by one on to the penthouse, so that they shall fulfil the conditions of a 'round service', practise 'striking out', cutting the ball, if possible, into the backhand corner of the opposite court. He must never forget that in order to play this stroke with effect, the ball must be between him and the side wall; if therefore he has misjudged its bound from the penthouse, and he finds that it is slightly in front of him, let him play it into the forehand corner, and, if it should be too far in front to admit of his playing for this stroke, he should boast it against the main wall into the backhand corner. Lastly, he should practise 'return', and will do well to secure the services of an intelligent marker who will play ball after ball to him with the precision of a catapult, and explain to him how and why the mistakes he most assuredly will make were caused. A few hours thus spent will help the beginner more than double the time occupied in playing with an unskilful, perhaps jealous, adversary, whose only wish may be to get the ball over the net somehow, and whose faulty style will be more easily imitated than avoided. I do not recommend the beginner to devote much time or attention to long fives, a game that is sometimes recommended as an excellent introduction to tennis. It is useful inasmuch as it develops facilities of return, but at the same time it is apt to encourage hard hitting and playing for nicks, instead of the classical style, which should be the object of attainment. I should, however, advise him to avail himself of any opportunity that may present itself of playing with an adversary who is strong enough to give him the odds of 'touch no walls'. Nothing is so improving to the young player as the return of balls that are coming towards him, and when these odds are given, this stroke must necessarily be repeated again and again in infinite variety.

Of the errors to which young players are prone, none is more common than a tendency to take the ball at the volley or the half volley when there is no necessity for so doing. A long hop can always be played more effectively than any other stroke, and it is generally better to step back and take the ball in its bound than to advance for the volley.

Beginners are also often too much addicted to forcing, tempted by the apparent facility of aiming accurately at so large an opening; but they should remember that direct forces are easily volleyed, and also that the penalty is a heavy one if the hazard is missed, for the ball must make a long chase or afford an opportunity of an easy stroke.

Moreover, that the difficulty of forcing straight is greater than it is supposed to be will be demonstrated by statistics, whose accuracy may be relied on, which were published in the *Field* in the summer of 1884. An analysis of strokes, which in the opinion of the reporter were forces, showed that of such strokes, Pettitt delivered 68 per cent that entered the dedans, or would have done so had they not been stopped; the present writer, 54 per cent; Mr A. Lyttelton, 40 per cent; and George Lambert 37 per cent only. The averages of the two last named players is lower than might have been expected, but it must be remembered that Mr Lyttelton seldom forces except in emergencies, and then with great severity, and that Lambert's favourite attack of the dedans is by that difficult stroke, the boast. Pettitt's average is a high one, but bearing in mind that no past or present player has played with accuracy for openings as he does, the inference may be drawn that play on the floor is not only the most classical but also the soundest.

It is not desirable to play constantly with one opponent. Although a contest with a strong antagonist encourages dash and severity, these qualities are cultivated at the expense of accuracy, and frequent play with a weaker opponent gives undue importance to a never failing, but perhaps weak, return.

I will now endeavour to point out to the young player, no longer a tiro, some of the countless variations of strategy that may be pursued by anyone who has mastered the first principles of the game. Let me suppose that he is matched with a player of around his own strength, and that he has the right to serve. He will probably have learned by experience that the 'side wall' service is the least fatiguing and most generally useful that he can deliver, so I will assume that he elects this well-known opening for his first attack. If the service is given with sufficient cut or overhand twist, and is also *bien ajuste*, the ball will cling so close to the end wall that his adversary will be compelled – unless he volleys it from the penthouse – to toss it high in the air so that it may bound into the dedans.

Some presence of mind is now required in calculating if it may be allowed to drop on to the floor, or if it must be volleyed. In the former case, it will be found easy to cut the ball into either corner of the court, but the latter alternative presents no opportunity for a decisive stroke. I should recommend the player, if the ball thus tossed comes to his forehand, to wait until it has dropped to within two feet or so from the floor, and to 'boast' it against the main wall to the opposite galleries; if it comes to his backhand, to take it at the level of his shoulder and to endeavour to place on or near the tambour.

If, however, the service is too short, i.e. if it does not reach the end wall, he will lay himself open to an attack in either corner of the court; if it is too long, i.e. if it strikes the end wall before the floor, an opportunity for a force, boasted or direct, or a stroke into the backhand corner, is afforded; and the server in both these cases will find himself put on his defence. If, therefore, he knows that his antagonist has learned that beautiful but hazardous stroke, the volley from the penthouse, or if he should be a striker out of more than average strength, he may think it best to attempt a more difficult opening, and assuming that he does not adopt that modern abomination the underhand twist in season and out of season, he cannot do better than give a drop service with some overhand twist. Another matter worthy of consideration is what service should be delivered when chases, long or short, must be defended. For yard chases it is, of course, of paramount importance that an opportunity for a 'force' should not be offered, and as balls coming towards a player are far less easily 'forced' than those that return from the end wall, a ball quietly tossed on to the penthouse, so that it shall drop on the floor near the galleries, will best meet the case. For the defence of chases worse than a yard and better than three, the 'giraffe' is useful; for others from three to the first gallery it is good policy to serve for a 'nick' with underhand twist; while if still longer chases, or chases on the hazard side, have been made, the 'drop' may prove a valuable resource.

The question is often asked, hat is the best service to which a player should resort after he has served one fault?' It is obvious that he must reduce to a minimum the chance of the delivery of a second fault, so the 'giraffe', or any fancy service, should be avoided, but any one may be selected that will combine some elements of difficulty with the certainty of its fulfilling the conditions of a good service. I have found it good policy to try for a nick, endeavouring rather to find the length of the court than to attain my object with the aid of twist.

I would caution the young player against too great eagerness while on the service side to return every ball. He should remember that if he changes sides to play for chase six, he has an advantage over his opponent, and that it is better to allow a long chase to be established than to attempt to return the ball without a fair prospect of deciding the 'rest'. The striker out, on the other hand, must return all strokes except those that would make hazard side chases, and the exigencies of the moment must determine if attack is possible, or what is the most aggressive form of defence open to him.

There is yet one question to which I would call the young player's attention: 'Where shall he place himself when his adversary has a *balle à la main*?' The grille, the last gallery, the tambour, and both corners of the court are all open to attack; which shall he try to defend?

Edmund Tompkins usually placed himself near the tambour, in a position that would enable him to volley any ball played to that part of the court; little, however, can be done with such a volley, and the rest of the court is deplorably open. George Lambert and Saunders adopt similar tactics, and both these players frequently make a successful counterattack, boasting the volley into the backhand corner. I prefer to stand in the middle of the court, taking my chance of my adversary's stroke being played upon the tambour, whence a beautiful return may often be made, prepared also to defend the forehand corner. I have observed that Pettitt occupies such a position, if so ubiquitous a player can be said ever to occupy any position in particular; and that Mr A. Lyttelton and most of our eminent amateurs adopt a similar system of defence.

6

The Origins of Lawn Tennis

Of the great family of sports and pastimes that fill up so large a part of English country life, lawn tennis is much the youngest member. Hunting, shooting and fishing, which in the nineteenth century are practised as fine arts, are nevertheless the developments of pursuits that owed their existence to the prime wants of savage nature. The elaborate coach with its team of thoroughbred horses is the lineal descendant of the humble manure-cart, to which the overburdened peasant first harnessed a donkey. Cricket looks back through a century of authentic history and ages of myth to its apocryphal commencement. Tennis has, for hundreds of years, been the sport of princes, a puzzle to the multitude, and the despair of nine-tenths of its votaries. Even golf, the newest madness of the moment, was chartered by royalty and practised by a little band of worshippers for two and a half centuries before, in these last days, it claimed a home on every common, forced a club into every hand, and deposited a ball in every bunker.

But lawn tennis is a new game. Viewed as an institution, that is, as a creature controlled by laws, based upon precedents, and protected by associations, it is barely in its teens. Its courts are hallowed by no historical incidents. The legends to which other sports pretend, and which in time ripen into accepted facts, are scanty and unsatisfying. No anecdotes of its precocious infancy can be gleaned by the inquiring chronicler, nor can even its pedigree be traced with the usual antiquarian accuracy through the various stages of its development from the elementary game of ball played by Nausicaa on the shores of Phaeacia to the Wimbledon tournament of the present year of grace. By many people, indeed, the game is supposed to have sprung like Minerva from the head of Jove, fully grown, and equipped with the newest pattern of racket, and the last championship ball, in or around the year 1874. This is far from being the case, nor is such a birth consistent either with experience or with the laws of nature. The production of a game, not less than the evolution of a species, presupposes a past of considerable duration, changes of more or less magnitude, and a stream of tendency more or less continuous in a given direction. Nor is this all. We shall expect to find some analogy between the infinitely great and the relatively little. The products of civilization have to pass through much the same phases as civilization itself has undergone. The experiences of the child are identical with those of the parent. We shall not be surprised to find in the history of a game the traces of a stage to which mankind in general has been compelled to submit, viz. the mythical epoch, of which the historian can say little more than that the events alleged to have taken place never had any real existence at all, being only beautiful tales embodying the dreams, the wishes and the aspirations of men. *Se non è vero è ben trovato*. Thence it passed into the legendary stage, when we have no longer to do with the region of pure myth, nor can we predicate with certainty in regard to any given incident that it could by no possibility have taken place. Fact and fiction are mixed up together, and the legend that comes down to us is a distorted and exaggerated representation of something that did actually take place. These two epochs in history correspond with the stages of lawn tennis prior to Major Wingfield's production of sphairistike, or, as the enemies of the newcomer called it, 'sticky'. The next stage is the anarchic or patriarchal age, when the local despot, represented, let us say, by the eldest brother at home during the university vacation, dictates to an obedient household or tribe the conventions, the decencies, the prescriptions, and laws of a narrow but sufficient civilization. Laws there are in abundance, but there is no correspondence between one tribal code and another, nor any subordination to a central authority. This is an age of heroes. The strongest and boldest warriors of each infinitesimal sept is in his own opinion, and that of those who surround him, the champion of the world; and in the absence of larger areas of competition, which will in a later age receive the name of championship tournaments, the local but very vulnerable Achilles, amid the plaudits of his village, drags down to the dust the reputation of a previously unconquerable Hector. But this stage also is transitory, and as it has been in history, so in lawn tennis it is followed by the monarchic period. The people will have a king to reign over them. The tribes, by conquest, mutual attraction, or otherwise, are compelled to coalesce. The longing for a settled government, as well as for easier means of intercourse with neighbours, creates a nation, and the nation, when created, bows down at the feet of the most powerful agent within itself, be it individual or association. So the scattered tribes and families of lawn tennis submitted themselves in the first instance to the Marylebone Cricket Club, and afterwards to other associations that will be described in their several places; and so this epoch also comes to an end, and the reign of law and order is inaugurated. But the march of intellect continues. The yearning for independence, the impatience of control not self-imposed, and the jealousy that autocratic power, though it be that of the Antonines, inspires, leads in time to an irresistible demand for representative government.

It is not home rule that is demanded, but federalism, in order to secure an equality of rights and a better adjustment of power, and thus the polity of lawn tennis passes at last into its final stage, and a republic of equal and co-ordinate clubs meeting in association is the supreme realisation of the aspirations that have swayed and directed the minds of lawn tennis players throughout the mythical, the legendary, the anarchic and the despotic eras in succession.

So far as this analogy holds good in respect to lawn tennis, the title of earliest lawgiver, as well as much of the credit of civilizing the game by introducing it to the notice of the public, is undoubtedly due to Major Wingfield, who in the year 1874, patented a game to which he gave the name of sphairistike; but the root must be sought much deeper, and conjecture may amuse itself by deriving the germs of Major Wingfield's game, and the main features of lawn tennis, from any or all of the pastimes that have preceded it, of which the principle has been the striking and returning of a ball or shuttlecock across a net or cord, whether by the agency of the hand, a battledore, or a racket, whether the game be called pallone, longue paume, handball, tennis, sphairistike, or badminton. The earlier notices of tennis would seem to indicate that it was played in the open air, and that the erection of courts was the invention of a later age. If this is so, lawn tennis may claim a higher dignity and a longer pedigree, while it loses the right to any merit on the ground of originality. Some form of out-of-door tennis seems to have been played almost from time immemorial, though the notices of it are so few and scattered as to suggest that its sporadic reappearances were experimental only, and failed to attract general interest. Towards the close of the last century, however, some such revival proved so popular that 'field tennis' is mentioned in the *Sporting Magazine* of September 1793, as a dangerous rival even to cricket. There are records of a similar game dating from around the year 1834, described under the name of 'long tennis' in a book entitled *Games and Sports*, being an appendix to *Manly Exercises* and *Exercises for Ladies*, by Donald Walker (Thomas Hurst, St Paul's churchyard, 1837). The Leamington Club claimed to have been acquainted with it for fifteen years before the revival by Major Wingfield, while it is said to have been played at Sir W. Scott's country seat, Ancrum in Roxburghshire, around the year 1864, as well as near Leyton around 1868. Lord Arthur Hervey, now Bishop of Bath and Wells, when the exigencies of his profession debarred him from his favourite game of tennis, had with his family and guests for many years played a substitute founded on tennis, and scored in tennis fashion, on the lawn of his rectory in Suffolk.

In more remote antiquity, even the patronage of Royalty is not wanting, for it is recorded that 'when Queen Elizabeth was entertained at Elvetham in Hampshire, by the Earl of Hertford, after dinner, about three o'clock, ten of his servants, Somersetshire men, in a square green court, before her Majestie's windows, did hangup lines, squaring out the form of a tennis court, and making a cross line in the middle; in this square they played, five to five, with handball, with bord and cord, as they tearme it, to the great liking of Her Highness' (Nicoll's *Progress of Queen Elizabeth*). It is probable that these instances might be largely increased by a diligent inquirer who should consider the search to be worth making. However that may be, it is certain that a species of lawn tennis, closely resembling in principle, if not in detail, that of the present day, had been for many years practised both in Russia and on a lawn here and there in this country, though it had taken no general hold on the public, taste. But for all practical purposes, it may be said that the epoch of lawn tennis dates from no more distant a period than 1874, when Major Wingfield resuscitated it by the introduction of sphairistike; so that, as compared with almost all other sports or games practised in England, it is still in its infancy. This infancy, however, was, like that of Hercules, one of extraordinary vigour. While still in the cradle, it strangled the rival games of sphairistike and badminton, and afterwards extinguished croquet as easily as the Greek hero crushed the Erymanthian boar. Something indeed of the rapidity with which lawn tennis superseded croquet must be attributed to a characteristic of the latter game that tended to smooth the path of the newcomer. The pastimes of England had been masculine games, and it had never been the custom for women to share in the sports of the country to as great an extent as they do at present. When croquet made its appearance, it was a new experience for women to be able to compete with men on tolerably even terms, and for sisters to partake in the amusements of their brothers with a fair chance of holding their own in the struggle. This feature, as well as the obvious social opportunities that croquet presented to all ages and to either sex, was a chief cause of its popularity. In default of a stronger attraction, a croquet lawn had become the indispensable adjunct to every country house, parsonage and villa, as well as a point of meeting and a sphere of rivalry to neighbours in every part of the kingdom. Trees that had been the delight of paterfamilias, and flower beds, which were to the mistresses of houses as the apple of an eye, had been ruthlessly removed to give scope for those passionate strokes that satisfied for the moment the vindictiveness of the most relentless croquet player. The turf of a thousand lawns – the gardener's pride and the neighbours' envy – condemned by young enthusiasts as too soft and mossy to allow the wooden ball to travel easily to its destined hoop, had been sacrificed to the exigencies of the momentary fashion, and had been replaced by a firmer and more lively surface, so that not only had social gatherings for the purpose of play become a necessary part of English life, but an arena to some extent fit for the purpose of lawn tennis existed already in every garden. Assisted perhaps by these circumstances, and recommended by its own inherent merits, lawn tennis made its way into popular favour with remarkable rapidity. Prior to the appearance of Major Wingfield's game, a species of outdoor tennis played on the grass may perhaps have been familiar to a few score of persons. By the summer of 1875, it had become universal; but though its worshippers were many, they were not of one creed. Methods were various, and laws were non-existent. This state of things could not continue, and, after much discussion and correspondence in the columns of the *Field*, a sub-committee of the Marylebone Cricket Club was deputed to frame a code. The task to which these gentlemen addressed themselves was a difficult one. They had to evolve order out of chaos, to formulate principles from imperfect analogies, and, with scanty experience to guide them, they were required to create a game. The code of the Marylebone Club was issued in 1875, and, though soon superseded, for the moment it served its purpose, which could not have been attained by any less authoritative organisation, of bringing into harmony a variety of discordant methods.

The need of some such paramount authority may be inferred from the circumstance that prior to the code, the court was of no prescribed length or breadth, while the height of the net and the position of the service line were a matter of discretion. At one time, indeed, the necessity of a service line was not universally admitted, and a competent judge once expressed an unhesitating opinion that any service dropping in its appropriate half court ought to be returned by a good player. Such was the state of anarchy when the MCC code appeared. Some measure of its utility is supplied by the fact that the length of the court has never since been altered, that it prescribed a definite height for the net, and maximum and minimum limits for the size and weight of balls, and, above all, introduced some uniformity of practice where, up to that time, every man, like the Israelite of old, had 'done that which was right in his own eyes'. In short, like Augustus, *'frena licentiæ injecit'*, if it cannot be added *'emovitque culpas'*, for alas, to eliminate faults from lawn tennis is as much beyond the power of any committee, however influential, as of the autocratic master of the Roman world.

7

The First Tournament

From what has been said it would appear that the origin of lawn tennis is to be sought, not so much in outdoor precursors or modifications of tennis, in pallone, longue paume, and similar pastimes, as in tennis itself, which, once known and enjoyed, does not easily lose its hold on its admirers. Debarred from the game they had loved and practised at university or in London, some few enthusiasts had, as we have seen, approached as nearly to their ideal as was possible under conditions.

There is, in fact, a form of tennis that in its essential features corresponds almost precisely with lawn tennis. It is now not often seen, though it is recommended to beginners as leading to the acquisition of return, and is known as 'long fives'. It is, in fact, tennis without the embarrassing addition of 'chases', and must necessarily have been known to every tennis player. In speaking, therefore, of the discovery or invention of Major Wingfield, the word is convenient rather than strictly accurate. It is possible, indeed, that Major Wingfield had seen, and perhaps taken part in, one of these occasional resuscitations of tennis. His merit consists in the fact that he was the first to realise that there was, in what he had seen or heard, a capacity of adaptation to the needs of society; and this is probably as much as can be said for the claim to originality of any inventor, however distinguished, or any discovery, however valuable.

The specification deposited by Major Wingfield with a view to obtaining a patent is dated 23 February 1874, and declares the invention to be 'a new and improved portable court for playing the ancient game of tennis'. The patentee explained the principle of his invention to be the erection of two standards, 21 feet apart, with an oblong net between them. Triangular nets forming side walls to the court were to be placed at right angles to the oblong net on each side; there were to be also a serving crease, in and out courts, right and left courts, and boundaries, marked with paint, coloured cord, or tape. Such was the description, and a diagram was appended showing the position of the net, wing nets, and lines marking the court and serving crease. There is a curious discrepancy between the description and the diagram. From the former, it is obvious that the court was intended to be rectangular, as the wing nets were to be at right angles to the oblong net; but in the diagram the court is delineated as wider at the baseline than at the net. Still, it is clear that Major Wingfield intended his game to be in accordance with the diagram, and he at all times claimed the 'hourglass shape' as one of the main principles of his invention. A month later, a few short and simple rules were published apparently by the authority of Major Wingfield, though not in his name; but for the most part they are definitions of the court rather than rules of play. They do not state in terms that the court was to have the hourglass shape, but from image 24 on p. 112 it appears that this must have been the case. The court was to be 20 yards long by 10 wide at the baselines. One side of the net, which was to be 4ft 8in. high, was the 'in' or serving court, and this was not divided by any lines; but in the centre of it, not far from the net, was a lozenge-shaped 'service crease', in which the server was to stand. In the 'out' court, a service line was to be drawn, the distance from the net being undefined, and the space between the service line and the baselines was divided into two equal courts, and the ball was to be served alternately into these courts. It is to be observed that the modern method of serving is the exact reverse of that proposed in Major Wingfield's rules. The illustration referred to is roughly reproduced, omitting certain trees and shrubs introduced in the original by the artist, which were probably designed to aid the pictorial effect, but which in practice would have constituted hazards of a most effective description. These hazards, for whatever purpose introduced, have at least proved prophetic, for on countless lawns, otherwise perfect, encroaching shrubs have been blessed or anathematised as in turn they either served the purpose of the server or impeded the stroke of the striker out.

It is singular that a game that has proved to be essentially one for the summer should at the outset have been specially recommended to the public as capable of being played on ice. Many attempts have been made in this direction, but they have met with little success. Nor is the reason hard to find. Lawn tennis balls do not bounce well upon ice, but even were it otherwise, lawn tennis and ice are not adapted to each other. The better a man skates, the less likely is he to succeed in playing lawn tennis upon ice, unless he reduces himself to the level of the inferior performer who is content to shuffle about on the flat of his skates. In truth, it can hardly be otherwise, at least in England, where the upright position, the unbent knee, and large, flowing curves are the essential elements of good skating, while lawn tennis requires absolute flexibility and quick irregular movement. The highest merit of either pursuit is a positive defect in the other. Quite apart, however, from the risk of transporting the infant game to an alien and incompatible element, there were many dangers to be surmounted, and many enemies, for the most part appearing in the guise of friendship, to be overcome. It was in danger of 'over-coddling' by one set of self-constituted nurses, who apprehended risk from the slightest breath of criticism, while another set were perhaps over-anxious to invest it with the full privileges of manhood before it had learned to walk alone. While eager partisans on the one hand piteously entreated that the game might not be spoiled, as had been the case with croquet, by the introduction of rules 'complicating it, and destroying its present pleasing simplicity which any fellow can understand', another faction was imperiously demanding legislation, without which they maintained that the precocious infant was likely to die of inanition. Meanwhile, 'the author was claiming that his invention should at least be preserved from the contaminating influence of tennis and rackets. This state of things was terminated by a proposal from Mr R. A. Fitzgerald, the honourable secretary of the Marylebone Cricket Club, to the effect that a meeting of lawn tennis players should be held at Lord's, in order to draw up a code that might obtain at least a provisional acceptance. The meeting was held early in 1875, and the

Tennis Committee of the Marylebone Cricket Club were requested to frame rules. On 24 May, the new code was issued under the sanction of the names of Hon. Spencer Ponsonby Fane, Hon. E. Chandos Leigh, Hon. C. G. Lyttelton, W. Hart Dyke, Esq., and J. M. Heathcote, Esq. In substance it provided that the court be divided into two equal parts by posts 7ft in height, and 24ft apart, with a net 5ft high at the posts and 4ft high at the centre. Baselines 30ft in length were to be drawn at a distance of 39ft, and service lines at a distance of 26ft from the net. The players were to be distinguished as 'hand-in' and 'hand-out'. Hand-in alone could serve, or score; and on losing a stroke he became hand-out. The service was to be delivered with one foot outside the baseline, and was required to drop between the net and the service line of the court diagonally opposite to that in which the server stood. If he failed to serve the ball over the net, he lost the stroke and became hand-out, but it was a fault only if the ball dropped in the wrong court or over the service line. The balls were to be 2¼in. in diameter and 1⅓oz. in weight. The game was fifteen up, as in rackets, but instead of being 'set' at fourteen all, the score was to be called deuce, then advantage, as in tennis. In double matches, the partner of the striker out might take a service dropping in the wrong court. Thus, it will be seen that the hourglass shape claimed by Major Wingfield as his special invention was adopted by the Marylebone Cricket Club, and Major Wingfield on his part cordially accepted the new rules.

This code, valuable as it was at the time, was short-lived, and hardly any matches are recorded as having taken place under it. It was probably adopted in a handicap match, reported as having been played at Cambridge in the month of June 1875, which was won by H. Leaf, Esq., late a Harrow boy, the first, but, as will be seen, by no means the last, success achieved as the result of practice at soft or 'squash' ball rackets at that school. In the early days of the game, the ball had been almost, if not quite, universally uncovered, but on 5 December 1874, a letter appeared in the *Field*, signed J. M. Heathcote, stating that the writer had found advantage in covering the balls with white flannel, which made them bound better, while they were also easier to see and to control. One of these balls used at Conington Castle, in Huntingdonshire, in the autumn of 1874, is still in existence, and though rude and archaic in construction, is undoubtedly the direct lineal ancestor of the latest and most improved championship ball.

Meanwhile, the growing popularity of the game is attested by many circumstances. In the year 1875, lawn tennis – mainly by the instrumentality of Mr Henry Jones, widely known as 'Cavendish' – was introduced into the programme of the All England Croquet Club, whose ground, situated at Wimbledon, a little to the west of the south-western railway station, has ever since been the headquarters of the game. The members of Prince's Club, Hans Place, had also adopted it, and were indeed so far in advance of their generation as to propose the lowering of the net to 3 feet. In the same year, too, was fulminated in the *Field* the first denunciation of the practice of volleying at the net, a practice that is condemned as 'unscientific', though a simple remedy for it is suggested in the widening of the net. In 1876, too, the adoption of tennis scoring was for the first time publicly advocated by Mr H. Jones, on the ground that thereby the interest is better sustained and handicapping facilitated. In the same year, the diffusion of the game is proved by a record of play by the English colony at Homburg. In short, lawn tennis was by this time established in public favour as an agreeable pastime and an excuse for pleasant social gatherings. But a graver crisis was at hand, which should determine whether the game was to bask for a few seasons in the smiles of fashion, and then decay and die, as rinking had done, and as croquet was destined to do; or whether it was to take its place permanently among recognised English sports, and so contribute to the formation of English character and English history.

This crisis is so important that it deserves more than a passing notice. The All England Croquet Club, of which Mr J. H. Walsh, the editor of the *Field*, was then honourary secretary, had already added lawn tennis to its original object. Early in 1877, the committee determined to make it in name as well as in fact a lawn tennis club, and it was accordingly for a short time designated as the All England Croquet and Lawn Tennis Club, until in a year or two all mention of croquet was dropped, and it became a lawn tennis club pure and simple. A few weeks later, the committee of the A. E. C. and L. T. Club announced that a lawn tennis championship meeting would be held at Wimbledon in the month of

July. Mr J. H. Walsh had induced the proprietors of the *Field* to offer for competition a silver challenge cup of the value of twenty-five guineas. If of late years, many a local committee has been able to offer more costly prizes, a special and almost sacred value will, in the opinion of lawn tennis enthusiasts, forever be attached to the trophy that, in the infancy of the game and amid all the uncertainties that necessarily surround a new and difficult experiment, the generosity of the *Field* newspaper and the energy of Mr Walsh enabled the committee of the A. E. C. and L. T. Club to offer to the lawn tennis players of England. Chief among these uncertainties and difficulties was the question of rules. No important match had been hitherto played, nor had any tournament been conducted under the MCC code. The committee of the A. E. C. and L. T. Club, while fully aware of the grave imperfections of that code, cannot but have been sensible of the serious danger incurred by a deviation from it. A vehement controversy had been maintained in the press on the relative merits and demerits of racket and tennis scoring respectively; nor was this the only topic for acrimonious discussion. The size of the court, the height of the net, the position of the service line, the question of faults, had been argued at great length and with considerable bitterness, and yet unanimity seemed as hopeless as ever. Prudence may have dictated an adherence as conservative as possible to the old lines, but the committee acted on a bolder and, as it has proved, a wiser instinct. Three gentlemen, Mr Julian Marshall, Mr Henry Jones, and Mr C. G. Heathcote, were appointed as sub-committee with the power to frame rules for the conduct of the championship meeting. Of these, Mr Marshall and Mr Jones had been the most prominent champions of the newer philosophy, and if their arguments were sharply controverted at the time, they had not been without effect. Compared, indeed, with the MCC code, the new rules might appear revolutionary; but the public was, in fact, prepared for revolution, and in the course of a few weeks, the unqualified success of the championship meeting disarmed, if it could not altogether extinguish, criticism. The principles of the new departure were :

1. A rectangular court 26 yards long by 9 yards wide, the net being suspended from posts placed 3ft outside the court.

2. The adoption of tennis scoring in its entirety.
3. The allowance of one fault without penalty, whether the service dropped in the net, in the wrong court, or beyond the service line. These principles have stood the test of time, and are still law. The MCC code was followed in respect of the service line, which was still to be 26ft from the net, and of the position of the server with one foot outside the baseline, two matters in which experience has shown a necessity for change, as has also been the case in regard to a service touching the net, which for the purpose of the moment was declared good. The height of the net was fixed at 5ft at the posts and 3ft 3in. at the centre, and a limit was prescribed to the balls of not less than 2¼in. nor more than 2⅝in. diameter, and of 1¼oz. to 1½oz. weight. In these respects experience has also dictated a change.

Such, without going minutely into details, were the conditions under which the first lawn tennis championship of England was decided. There were twenty-two competitors, of whom many were more or less familiar with tennis scoring, a circumstance that was perhaps fortunate for the legislators, as it prevented the expression of any marked dissatisfaction with the rules. Mr Henry Jones acted as referee, but the machinery worked so smoothly that few difficult questions were submitted to him. The posts, nets and balls were supplied by Messrs Jefferies & Co., of Woolwich. The number of entries necessitated byes in the second and fourth rounds, as well as a supplementary match to decide the winners of the second and third prizes. The all-corners prize and the Championship were won by Mr Spencer Gore, an old Harrovian and racket player; the second and third prizes being secured by Messrs W. C. Marshall and C. G. Heathcote respectively, who were both tennis players. Mr Gore had previously defeated Mr M. Hankey and Mr F. Langham, who had been proficient as tennis players, and whose style was modelled on that game. So far, therefore, as the result of one experiment could decide the question, the racket style appears thus early to have given proof of the superiority, which it has maintained ever since. In Mr W. C. Marshall, Mr Gore undoubtedly met and easily vanquished a strong exponent of the tennis style, but it is probable that among the ranks of professed tennis players one or two might have been found who, if they could have been induced to take up lawn tennis seriously, might have given the champion more trouble. As it was, Mr Gore was much the best player of the year. He was gifted with a natural genius for all games, great activity, a long reach, and a strong and flexible wrist. In addition to these natural advantages, he was emphatically a clever player, and created a game of his own that, had he not very early abandoned match playing, would have proved capable of easy adaptation to altered circumstances. Doubtless the volley has become in other hands a much more powerful attacking force, but Mr Gore's volley, which was his own creation, was no mere pat over the net. He was the first to realise, as the first and great principle of lawn tennis, the necessity of forcing his opponent to the back line, when he would approach the net, and by a dexterous turn of the wrist would return the ball at considerable speed, now in the forehand and now in the backhand court, till, to borrow the expression of one of his best opponents of that year, his antagonist was 'ready to drop'. Though the hard overhand service was not then invented, his service was more varied than that of almost all other players, and his underhand service in particular was characterised by an extraordinary power of twist. However great may have been the talents of Mr Gore's successors in the championship, those who recollect his play will assign him a very high place among players, especially when they remember how original he was in his method, and how little in the way of tradition or example contributed to its conception or development

8

The Development of Lawn Tennis

The first lawn tennis championship match was over, the shouts that greeted the victor had subsided, the secretary had noted with satisfaction the facility with which his club might recruit an exhausted exchequer with the shillings and half crowns of a public eager for novelty, the adherents of the old method of scoring were half converted by the successful working of the new system; but, in spite of these triumphs, or perhaps by reason of them, so far from reposing in contentment on the merits of the recent rules, critics at once began to discover in them grave defects and important omissions. The most serious of these was the great preponderance of the service. Mr H. Jones, from analysis of the scoring cards, states that of 601 games played in the tournament, the server had won 376 to 225 won by the striker out, in other words, a proportion in favour of service of five to three; or, if only the more even sets were chosen for comparison, of nine to five. If the modern fast overhand service with the lowered net had been in vogue at this time, the undue preponderance of service would have been even more marked; but the players for the most part delivered a roundhand service that, though it had some pace, was far less formidable. Yet, as it was, the mere statement of the statistics made it evident that service was far too powerful. Three remedies presented themselves as obvious: to heighten the net in the middle; to penalise a single fault; or to bring the service line nearer to the net. Of these alterations, a considerable body of partisans preferred the penalisation of the first fault, while the All England Club advocated the course, shortly afterwards adopted, of bringing in the service line. This was effected early in 1878 by a joint code of laws issued by the MCC and the All England Club. The height of the net was reduced to 4ft 9in. at the posts and 3ft at the centre, and the service line was placed at a distance of 22ft from the net. The dimensions of the court, as adopted at Wimbledon, were preserved, and all idea of the hourglass shape was finally dismissed. For the three-handed and four-handed games, a width of 12 yards was prescribed, thus obviating the necessity of keeping the single and double courts distinct, an arrangement that on private lawns has proved very convenient. The weight of the balls was fixed at 2 oz., a somewhat excessive amount that has not been retained; but in most other respects, these laws were almost identical with the rules framed by the All England Club for their own meeting, except that the MCC, with a truly conservative instinct, retained as an alternative the racket method of scoring, and in successive revisions of their rules continued to do so until 1883, when the alternative method was definitively abandoned. In 1878, there was some reason for retaining it, as in the previous year several matches had been scored on that principle, including a four-handed tournament at Prince's Club in June, one at Deddington in August, and one held by the Wirral Club in October. It was, however, rarely employed afterwards, and long before 1883, had become wholly obsolete. Under the joint rules of the two clubs (excepting, of course, the alternative method), the second All England Championship meeting was held in July 1878. Thirty-four competitors entered, of whom the most eminent were Messrs P. F. Hadow, L. Erskine, E. B. Brackenbury, A. T. Myers, C. G. Hamilton, who in tennis had successfully represented the University of Cambridge in that year against Oxford, Mr H. F. Lawford, whose name is now so well known in the lawn tennis world, but who on this occasion made his first public appearance, and the Honourable G. Montgomerie. The most exciting match was that between Messrs Erskine and Hamilton, who in the fourth round played five sets, the last of which on more than one occasion depended on a single stroke. The championship match produced a keen struggle between Mr Hadow, who had in the preliminary rounds defeated all his antagonists without losing a set, and Mr S. Gore, the champion of the previous year, and resulted in the victory of Mr Hadow by three sets to love. It is no disparagement to the winner to add that Mr Gore was suffering from a sprained wrist, which must have placed him at a disadvantage. Mr Hadow, like his predecessor, had been a Harrow boy, and was proficient at rackets. Without much severity either of service or stroke, he placed with great accuracy, and displayed a certainty of return they had not been hitherto equalled, and perhaps has hardly ever been excelled. If he did not invent the lob, he was the first to practise it with any great success, and he met and vanquished Mr Gore's tactics by a free use of this resource. Mr Hadow shortly afterwards left England for Ceylon, and has not appeared again in important matches. Mr Erskine took the second prize, and Mr Lawford the third. Those who of late years have seen and appreciated the 'suddenness, the accuracy, and the terrible speed of Mr Lawford's strokes' will, perhaps, be surprised to learn that at this time the second of these qualities was alone remarkable – a proof, if any were needed, that a strong game can only be built up by slow degrees and by much patient perseverance. The result of the analysis of service showed that of 431 games played by good or fairly equal players, 229 were won by the server, and 202 by the striker out, the advantage of service being around 8½ to 7½. This result was considered satisfactory, and no further change in the service line was for the time considered necessary. It is clear, however, that already the volleyer at the net had given rise to a burning question. Not only did he stand persistently close to the net, and frequently kill the best strokes of his opponent, but occasionally he invaded the territory of his adversary and volleyed the ball before it had passed the net. An instance had indeed occurred in the championship match of 1878. It was proposed on the one hand that a penalty should be imposed on touching the net in striking, while others wished to limit the possibility of volleying at the net by the addition of a volleying line, within which the player was not to stand, while others even desired to prohibit the practice altogether. These remedies were objected to, as adding to the burden of the already overweighted umpire; but this argument was overruled, and so far as finality in such a matter can be predicated, the question has been finally disposed of by a rule forbidding a player to volley a ball before it has passed the net. The point has been so far important in the history of the game that it gave rise to the first suggestion that an association of lawn tennis clubs, consisting of fifty members or upwards, should be convened specially to prohibit the practice. Hitherto, as we have seen, there had been hardly any open tournaments, but the success of the two All England meetings had paved the way for others, and early in the year 1879, it was announced that the Oxford University Lawn Tennis Club had instituted a four-handed championship, and had offered a cup, the competition for which took place in May, when the trophy was won by Messrs L. R. Erskine and H. F. Lawford. In this year also was inaugurated the championship of Ireland, played in Dublin, and repeated with ever increasing prestige in each successive year to the present time. The prize was won by Mr V. Goold, at that time better known by the name of 'St Leger', under which he played. The meeting was further remarkable as being the first occasion on which ladies competed for a championship, which on this occasion was secured by Miss M. Langrishe, whose name occurs frequently in lawn tennis annals.

A proof of the increasing popularity of the game, as well as of the general belief that the possibility of success was not at that time limited, as is now the case, to three or four well-known players, is furnished by the fact that there were forty-five competitors for the All England Championship of 1879, of whom only nine had taken part in previous contests at Wimbledon. Mr P. F. Hadow, the holder, being in Ceylon, could not defend his title; but the list, in addition to Messrs Erskine and Lawford, the second and third prizewinners of the preceding year, included Messrs W. Renshaw, E. Renshaw, A. J. Mulholland, O. E. Woodhouse, E. Lubbock, C. F. Parr, V. Goold, the Irish champion, C. D. Barry, who had taken second honours at Dublin, and J. T. Hartley, who, though quite unknown at Wimbledon, came up from Yorkshire with a great reputation. Of these, the two Renshaws were prevented from putting in an appearance, but the absence of two young men of eighteen years of age was hardly noticed at the time amid the host of competitors, and no forecast could at that time be made of their coming greatness. At the end of the six rounds made necessary by the large number of entries, Mr J. T. Hartley emerged the winner, like his predecessors an old Harrovian, but unlike them a tennis player who had represented Oxford in 1870. His closest struggle was in the second round against Mr L. R. Erskine, but the practice he obtained in his earlier matches was of the highest value to him, and when on the final day he met and vanquished Mr V. Goold, he was undoubtedly a much stronger player than he had been on the occasion of his first match on the All England ground a week before. The result of the play was summed up by a writer in a daily paper: 'Safety is the first requisite in lawn tennis, and brilliancy the second.' This remark, from which as a general proposition large deductions should be made, was certainly true of the tournament of 1879. The showy and more attractive style of Mr Goold, with all its brilliancy, could achieve no success against the unfailing judgment that was the most conspicuous characteristic of Mr Hartley's game. The French proverb, '*la balle cherche le bon joueur*', might indeed be applied to the lawn tennis champion of 1879. It was not so much he who went after the ball as the ball that went after him. The accuracy of his return, too, was equal to that of his judgment, and though tested by modern standards he might not be classed as a hard hitter, he nevertheless made the ball travel at a good pace. Seldom volleying himself, he would repeatedly defeat the tactics of a volleyer by passing him in the most dexterous manner. In short, he was more accurate than hard hitters, and hit harder than the accurate players of his day, and this combination of qualities secured for him a victory that was as popular as it was unexpected. Mr V. Goold took the second and Mr Parr the third prize. It may have been owing to accidental circumstances or to the prevailing type of play, that service in this tournament more than maintained its old supremacy, the analysis showing that, with the service line unaltered and excluding hollow matches and those played on one day when the wind was excessive, service won 352 games and lost 295, a proportion of about eleven to nine, while the strokes won by the server were to those won by the striker out in the proportion of twenty-four to twenty-three. Among many curious suggestions made about this time for doing away with the anomalies inseparable from the existing method of scoring, one is sufficiently remarkable to deserve notice. It was proposed that lawn tennis should be scored as whist is marked – that a love game should be represented by a treble or three points, a game in which the loser scored fifteen or thirty should constitute a double or two points, and that when deuce or advantage should have been reached, the winner should score a single or one point. The set was to consist of twenty points, and the match would be decided by the aggregate of points instead of by an aggregate of sets. It is hardly necessary to add that this ingenious scheme met with little support, but its leading principle of scoring by points has since been not unfrequently suggested, and it would be rash to affirm that in some form it may not be again revived. One more open tournament was played in this year that may be mentioned as first introducing the Messrs Renshaw to public notice. It was played at Cheltenham in October, partly outdoors on asphalt and partly in a covered court, and was won by Mr W. Renshaw, who defeated Mr V. Goold. The estimate formed of the winner by the reporter of this match has been amply justified: 'With more experience he will give trouble to the best players in the kingdom. He is most active in the court, and seldom misses a return'; 'but,' the chronicler adds, 'his stroke is not severe'. In this respect only, the statement will at the present day appear to require modification.

Before the close of 1879, Mr J. Walsh, who as honourary secretary of the All England Club had been indefatigable in the cause of lawn tennis and had rendered to the game services of the highest value, resigned his office, which was shortly afterwards filled by the appointment of Mr J. Marshall. This gentleman sustained the difficult burden of management with conspicuous success for nearly nine eventful years, during which the history of the legislation of lawn tennis may be said to have been virtually the history of the club he served, and he retained office until the spring of 1888, when the All England Club was about to resign into the hands of a Central Association the initiative which it had exercised from the commencement of the game, and to transfer the legislative functions of the club to a wider and more representative body. Those who were most closely associated with Mr Marshall in his arduous labours, if on the one hand they may be in some measure biased by partiality, will yet be best able to appreciate his untiring energy and great services in the cause of the game in the promotion of which he took so large a part.

The lawn tennis season of 1880 was heralded by the institution of the Northern Lawn Tennis Association, and preceded by a revision of the laws by the Marylebone and All England clubs. The code as then issued was substantially that in use at the present day, with two exceptions, viz., that the height of the net at the posts was fixed at 4ft, a height that has since been further reduced to 3ft 6in., and the server, though compelled to deliver the service as now with one foot beyond (further from the net than) the baseline, was allowed an option of having the other foot either within or upon it. He is now compelled to serve with one foot upon and the other behind the baseline. Additions to and explanations of the laws of 1880 have indeed been at various times inserted, but without making any vital alteration, and with the two exceptions above, the laws of 1890 are in substance the laws of 1880. By this revision, the service line was brought in to a distance from the net of 21ft, the limits of variation in the size and weight of the balls was fixed, a service not delivered in accordance with the laws was declared a fault, a service touching the net if otherwise good was declared to count for nothing, the player was forbidden under penalty of losing the stroke to touch the net or to volley the ball before it had passed the net, and on application by either party before tossing for choice, the umpire might direct the players to change sides after each game. Such were the principal novelties in the single game; but in the four-handed game a very important change was effected by the introduction of service sidelines, by which the strength of service was materially reduced. In the ensuing month of May, on the occasion of the four-handed championship held as in the preceding year at Oxford, 'coming events' began 'to cast their shadows before' when Messrs W. and E. Renshaw by beating in succession Messrs A. J. and H. L. Mulholland, Messrs R. W. Braddell and J. Comber, and Messrs C. J. Cole and O. E. Woodhouse proved themselves for the first, but by no means for the last, time the best pair in England. Their service is described as not having been 'at any time very severe', but their volleying is considered to deserve especial praise, and it is evident from the report that they had by this time developed to a high degree of perfection what was afterwards called the 'Renshaw smash'. A few days later, Mr W. Renshaw carried off the Irish championship played in Fitzwilliam Square, Dublin, defeating successively Messrs R. T. Richardson, H. F. Lawford, M. G. McNamara, E. de S. Browne, and

V. Goold, the champion of the preceding year – no small achievement, considering that the winner was only nineteen years of age, and that his opponents were among the strongest players in England and Ireland. He was, however, unable to repeat his success in the championship match at Prince's Club, when, owing possibly to the slippery state of the ground, he was beaten by Mr Lawford. Messrs E. Lubbock, E. Renshaw, R. T. Richardson (who shortly afterwards won the Northern Association Championship), and O. E. Woodhouse also played in this tournament, and the final match in which Mr Lawford beat Mr Lubbock was rendered remarkable by the longest rest recorded in a first-class match, extending to eighty-one strokes. There was no diminution in the number of competitors for the All England Championship. They amounted to sixty, and comprised most of the best known players of the day. Mr Woodhouse, an unequal player, occasionally displaying great brilliancy, was seen at his best in his successive victories over the two Renshaws and the Hon. G. Montgomerie, but in the final match his weaker physique proved unable to cope with the indefatigable energy of Mr Lawford. The latter was unable to wrest the championship from the grasp of Mr Hartley, the holder, who won with apparent ease. In this match also, as at Prince's, the great length of the rests elicited an admiration not altogether unalloyed by weariness, one of thirty-three strokes, and four exceeding twenty-five, being recorded. Certainty of return indeed had been studied by the best players, with an assiduity that tended to impair the popularity, and even to threaten the very existence, of lawn tennis. It is true that no apparent diminution of interest on the part of the public could as yet be discerned. The 200 spectators who had found their way to the lawns of Wimbledon to witness the championship match of 1877 had grown to 700 in 1878, and 1,100 in 1879, while 1,300 people are said to have witnessed the triumph of Mr Hartley in 1880. The execution of the performers was incontestably more perfect than it had been three years earlier, but the interest of the performance was imperilled by its very success. A new crisis had arisen in the history of the game. It had survived ridicule, it had surmounted obloquy. It had long raised itself above the level of agreeable amusement, and had become a national institution, but monotony is a danger with which no game can successfully cope. With all its merits, it was still in the leading strings imposed by the traditions of tennis and rackets. Some originality indeed had been imparted to it by the versatile genius of Gore, the unerring judgment of Hartley, the unstudied grace of Goold; but in the hands of the majority of the most successful practitioners, its highest achievement was a perfect but mechanical precision. In the growth and progress of this precision, the earlier stages of the game found their object and their expression. How and by whose agency it asserted an individuality it had not previously possessed, in what manner it shook itself free from the trammels of tennis and rackets, and entered seriously on the development of distinct principles and tactics of its own, forms a branch of our subject that requires, as it deserves, a separate treatment.

9

The Revolution of Lawn Tennis

1881

In the history of games, instances present themselves, though but rarely, of some fortunate individual who has been able, by merit or accident, to alter the course or give direction to the tendency of the pastime that he professes, and thus to link his name indissolubly with its annals. Such a man in cricket was David Harris, the bowler, who by the rapid rise and puzzling curl with which he imparted to the ball enforced a more cautious style and a more upright bat, and contributed to the introduction by W. Fennex of forward play. Such men in billiards were Carr of Bath, who systematically applied, if he did not discover, the side stroke, and Peall, who by showing the world how the spot stroke could be indefinitely repeated brought about the elimination from first-class billiards of his favourite hazard. It is not necessarily the greatest player of his day who enjoys this supreme good fortune; and in all games names of the very highest eminence may be quoted whose possessors have never attained to it. Moreover, the longer an amusement has lasted, the more difficult does the task become, but when accomplished it is not so much a reform as a revolution. Such an event was at hand in 1881, though the men who were to lead it were almost entirely unknown. It is true that Messrs William and Ernest Renshaw had enjoyed a foretaste of their coming triumphs at Oxford and Dublin in the preceding year, and that they had then displayed much the same style as that which has since had so great an influence on the game; but the portent was watched by an unheeding world, and created no imitators. These were isolated victories, and at Prince's and Wimbledon success had rested with the exponents of the older style. It was possible that the new departure might prove only a broad way leading to destruction, the new and brilliant star might be but an *ignis fatuus* guiding into the dreary fens of disappointment, or the Serbonian bog of disaster. But the spring was not far advanced before the adherents of the old regime were compelled to bow to the logic of events. Mr E. Renshaw scored the first family victory of the year against Mr E. de S. Browne at Cheltenham in April, but the chief glories of the season were achieved by his brother, Mr W. Renshaw. The retention of the championship of Ireland, and the winning of Prince's and the All England championships, made the year a triumphal progress for the young player of twenty, while in four-handed matches he was equally successful in combination with his brother, the pair winning the championship matches both at Oxford and Dublin. They had already, at least tentatively, discarded the old practice in accordance with which one player would assume a position at the baseline, while the other stood near the service line, but apparently they were not, until much later, definitely convinced of the superiority of the new station, on or about the service line – for we shall find Mr W. Renshaw in a letter to the *Field* dated 26 May 1883, advocating the old method. At this time they were, indeed, trying experiments, which they may sometimes have found dangerous, but whichever position they adopted they were almost invariably successful. Even in single matches they were at this time to some extent experimentalising. They both indulged in the volley and in the smash to which they gave their name, to an extent frequently excessive and occasionally reckless, and their back play had not the severity it has since acquired. Hence, even up to the last moment before the Wimbledon meeting, it was thought by some that Lawford's powerful back play, Richardson's combination of restrained strength in volley with admirable certainty from the back of the court, or Hartley's accuracy and judgment, would prove superior to the brilliant but sometimes erratic power of the young aspirant. The result showed that those who so thought were wrong. Lawford, indeed, made an excellent fight, and was beaten only by the odd set; but Richardson offered only a feeble resistance, and the match with Hartley, owing to the illness of the latter, was concluded in thirty-seven minutes, and from its unnatural decisiveness was an

Above: 1. 'La Paume'.

Right: 2. Courts at the Louvre: a) the Guichet du Louvre, c) the Tour du Coin, d) the Arche d'Autriche, l) the Dépendence de l'Hôtel de Villeroy, n) the Mur d'enceinte de Philippe Auguste, oo) the Emplacement des Jeux de Paume.

Le chasteau du Louvre

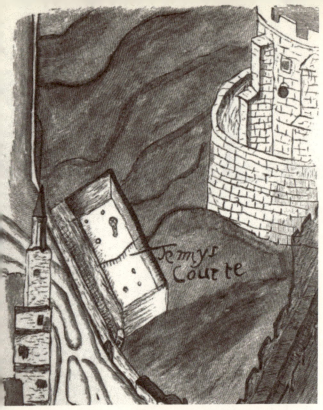

Left: 3. Tennis court at Windsor, AD 1607.

Below: 4. Tennis court at Hampton Court in the time of Henry VIII.

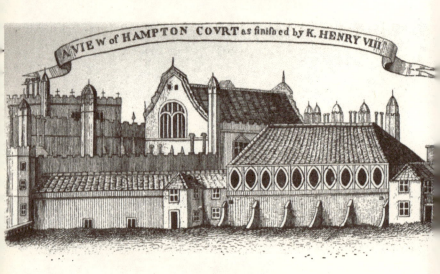

Above: 5. Tennis courts at Fontainebleau, AD 1614.

Below: 6. Fontainebleau.

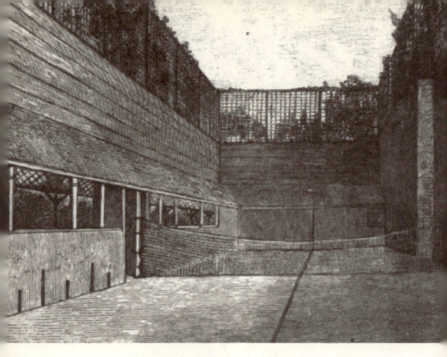

Above: 7. Mr Orchardson's tennis court at Westgate-on-Sea.

Left: 8. Rackets, AD 1675.

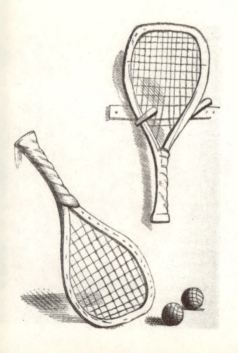

Left: 9. A racket, AD 1767.

Far left: 10. A racket, AD 1890.

Below: 11. Interior of tennis court, Queen's Club (seen hazard side).

Above: 12. Interior of tennis court, Queen's Club (seen from service side).

Left: 13. T. Pettitt delivering underhand twist services.

14. J. M. Heathcote cutting the ball fore-handed.

15. C. Saunders volleying the service from the penthouse.

16. J. M. Heathcote forcing fore-hand.

17. C. Saunders cutting the ball back-handed.

18. J. M. Heathcote half-volleying
fore-handed.

19. A. Lyttelton half-volleying
back-handed (from front).

Left: 20. A. Lyttelton half-volleying back-handed (side view).

Below: 21. Grasp of the racket for a fore-hand stroke.

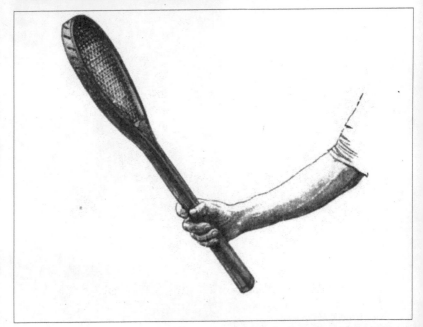

22. Grasp of the racket for a back-hand stroke

23. Tennis at home.

24. Diagram of Major Wingfield's game of Sphairistike.

Right: 25. The 'Caxton' lawn tennis marker.

Below left: 26. The 'Cavendish' post.

Below right: 27. The 'Championship' post.

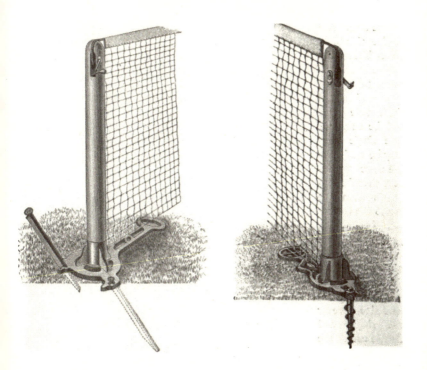

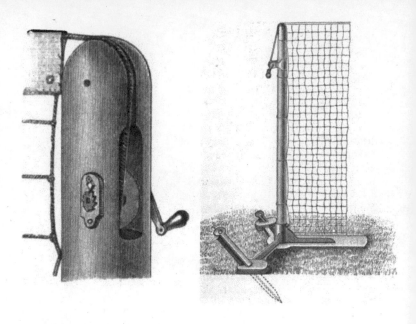

Above left: 28. Ratchet of the 'Cavendish' post.

Above right: 29. The 'Cyprus' post.

Right: 30. 'Cyprus' ratchet and winder.

Right: 31.
The racket.

Below left:
32. Hope's
umpire's seat.

Below right:
33. Abacus
scoring board.

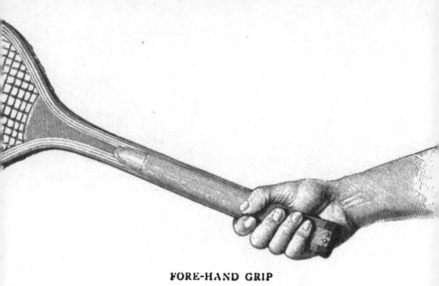

FORE-HAND GRIP

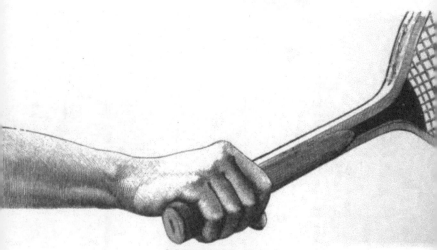

BACK-HAND GRIP

34. A fore-hand and back-hand grip.

35. Preparing for a
fore-hand stroke.

36. Preparing for a
back-hand stroke.

37. Overhand service.

38. The service.

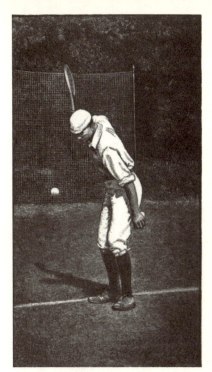

39. Fore-hand drive.

40. The drive.

41. Back-hand drive.

42. The smash.

43. Back-hand smash.

44. Smashing a lob.

45. Horizontal volley.

46. Fore-hand half-volley.

47. Back-hand
half-volley.

48. Back-hand
half volley.

Left: 49. Preparing to receive the service.

Below: 50. The four-handed game.

Opposite: 51. Lawn tennis court, 1874.

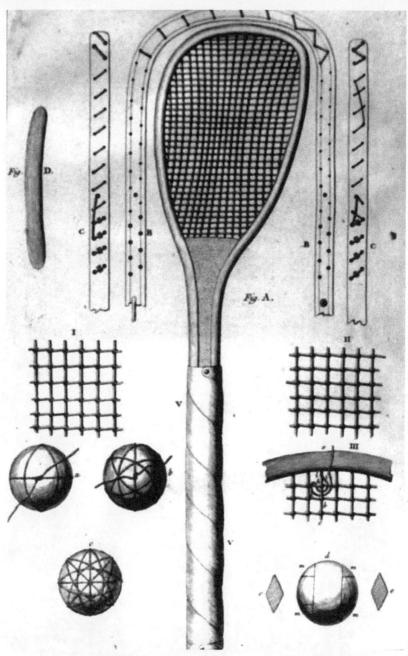

52. Creation of a tennis racket, eighteenth century.

utterly inconclusive test of the merits of the two styles. No one who witnessed the match, however, could have failed to agree with the frank admission of the vanquished champion that the back play of that date had had its day, and that victory *de jure* as well as *de facto* rested with the species of volley adopted by the winner. Everyone now knows the advantage of this method; everyone can see how much more of the net can be covered at the service line than at the net, how much easier it is to run forward than back, how much less distance has to be traversed if it is necessary to retreat, and how a *locus pœnitentiæ* is left to the player who has come up prematurely to the service line which is wanting to the player at the net; but little of all this was known in 1881, and the boldness and originality of the idea was no less remarkable than its sudden and startling success. The title of champion thus won in 1881 by Mr W. Renshaw was retained by him until 1887, when he retired owing to an injury to his arm, now widely known as tennis elbow, of which the first public mention is found in the columns of the *Field* in 1881. It is not impossible that Mr Renshaw, by the increased severity both of service and smash introduced by him at this time, and at once imitated by a host of players, may have contributed to the vastly increased prevalence of the injury, which has since, though fortunately only for a time, taken its revenge upon himself. Tennis elbow has generally been attributed to the great and sudden strain thrown upon the muscles of the arm by the overhand service, and though this service was not absolutely the creation of 1881, it was now delivered with vastly increased severity.

An interesting handicap was played at Prince's in June, in which Mr E. Renshaw received alike from his brother and from Mr Lawford the odds of two bisques, and just won both matches, so that the difference between the three players cannot have been great. In this match, the turf being wet, Mr Lawford wore shoes with small leather protuberances to prevent him from slipping. To this the management objected, and the immediate result of their decision may have been the loss of the match. Among the ulterior consequences was the introduction of steel points, now universally worn in wet weather. In the same month, the first matches took place between Oxford and Cambridge, the former being successful both in the singles and the four-handed matches. Two other tournaments may be mentioned, not as remarkable in themselves, but as showing the wide diffusion of the game. The first took place at Durban in Natal, the other at a height of 6,000ft above the sea, on or near the top of Mount Troodos or Olympus in Cyprus, then the summer quarters of the British troops. A spirited attempt was also made to play the game by electric light at Cheltenham in December; an attempt that has since been repeated, but without much success. On this occasion, the Brush system was adopted, and the experiment was so far satisfactory that the result was not a matter of mere chance, and the match was won by the best player, Mr W. Renshaw, with Miss Bradley as his partner. No ladies' championship had as yet been instituted at Wimbledon, nor was any such match played in this year at Dublin, but Miss G. R. Gibbs at Bath, Miss Bradley at Cheltenham, Miss Cole at Exmouth, and Miss M. Watson at Edgbaston, respectively evinced their superiority to their rivals.

Among the debutants of the year were Mr E. L. Williams, then only fifteen years of age, Mr C. W. Grinstead, and Mr H. Grove, each of whom has since had a distinguished career. These three gentlemen, as well as a number of eminent players who will be mentioned hereafter, formed their style and mode of attack upon that of the Renshaws. A standard of play had thus been introduced to which nearly every promising beginner conformed; a school had been formed in which every tiro enrolled himself as a disciple, and it is this circumstance, even more than the brilliancy of the play, that makes the year 1881 an epoch in lawn tennis.

1882

As has happened in revolutions of a still more important character, the negation of established principles and the removal of old landmarks were succeeded by a reign of terror. Players and public alike, inspired by the success and universality of the volley, had indeed revolted against interminable rests consisting entirely of strokes from the back of the court; but they were not less strenuously opposed to the introduction of a game that should differ from battledore and shuttlecock principally in the shortness of the struggle. Was lawn tennis to be reduced to the interchange of three or four sharp repartees from the service line, followed by a smash from the vicinity of the net? One player, and one alone, of first-class position, had hitherto resisted the contagion of the volley. Mr Lawford had played consistently and with ability from the back of the court, but he had been beaten; and it seemed certain that under the existing conditions the volley must be taken to have a definite and constant superiority. The Marylebone and All England clubs resolved, therefore, on 12 May 1882, to meet the difficulty by lowering the net at the posts from 4ft to 3ft 6in. It was a small modification, and both the principle of the change and the time for effecting it were warmly impugned. Time and experience have amply vindicated the wisdom of the decision. Its first results were seen in the four-handed game in a temporary but decided check to the service line position. Messrs W. and E. Renshaw failed to retain the championship of Ireland at Dublin, and that of England at Oxford. In the former they were defeated by Messrs E. de S. Browne and P. Aungier, and in the latter by Messrs Hartley and Richardson.

On both occasions the winners adhered to the older method, where the back player would find his position strengthened by the increased facility of playing down the sidelines in consequence of the change in the law, the skill in this respect of Mr Hartley, who in the Oxford match took the back play exclusively, being especially noted in the contemporary reports. A second result of equal importance was soon observable. At the championship meeting at Wimbledon, in the match between Messrs E. Renshaw and Lawford, the server won seventeen games only, while the striker out secured twenty-six, and when Mr E. Renshaw met Mr Richardson, the striker out won twenty-three games to fourteen won by the server. It is obvious that with the lower net, service, however fast, could be returned at greater speed and with more accuracy along the sidelines; and thus, though severer than ever, it had lost its ascendency. The new law did not, however, materially affect results in the single game. The twin brothers were as successful in this as they had been in the preceding year. Mr E. Renshaw, after defeating all his opponents at Dublin, declined to challenge his brother for the championship, and at Wimbledon the same two players were left to compete for the premiership of lawn tennis, and the holder, though not without a severe struggle, retained his position. Next to these the most successful players of the year were Mr R. T. Richardson and Mr E. de S. Browne, both in the main volleyers, and Mr Lawford, who still restricted himself chiefly to back play, and under the altered conditions had perhaps not had time to bring to perfection his most formidable attack from baseline to baseline along the sides of the court. Oxford again beat Cambridge in both the annual lawn tennis events, a result that might have been expected from the fact that Messrs Grinstead, H. Grove, J. G. Horn and C. B. Russell were included in the winning teams. Mr E. L. Williams created a sensation by beating Mr E. de S. Browne at the Agricultural Hall, and names new to lawn tennis are recorded in Messrs Donald Stewart, H. W. Wilberforce, and E. W. Lewis, who for the first time obtained success destined to be often repeated. Of the ladies, Miss Abercromby at Dublin, Miss F. Morris at Bath, and Miss M. Langrishe at the Northern meeting were eminently successful.

1883

For some time past, a feeling had been growing in favour of a more direct representation of lawn tennis players in general in matters connected with the game. It had been fostered by the diffusion of first-class play in the provinces, by the vast increase in the number of clubs, and the improvement of the standard of play. Accordingly, early in 1883, a meeting to discuss the formation of a Lawn Tennis Association was held in London, but the result was inconclusive. A proposal was made and carried that a conference should be held with the All England Club on the subject. That club, in declining the conference, offered to institute an annual meeting of secretaries of clubs with power to arrange fixtures and to discuss matters affecting the game; and a second meeting for the discussion of the question of association negatived the project by a very small majority. The offer of the All England Club was then accepted, and thenceforth until 1888 a meeting of lawn tennis representatives was annually held under the presidency of the secretary of the All England Club.

Meanwhile, the reaction against the volleyer continued. The assistance of legislation was invoked. The offender was to be abolished altogether, or at least to be ostracised from the vicinity of the net, and fears were expressed that 'if the present system were kept up lawn tennis would fall more and more into the hands of a few first-class players'. In short, the saviour of society of two years before had become the enemy of the human race. Still, in spite of denunciation, he pursued his course. He did more, he threatened a further advance, a more exclusive superiority. We find Mr Renshaw predicting that 'before many years taking the ball off the ground will be quite the exception; and in its place there will be far finer and more exciting rallies in the volley than have ever been up to the present'. On the other hand, Mr Lawford writes that 'perfect back play will beat perfect volleying. It is always possible to pass a volleyer with the court as it is at present; and I know that when I lose a stroke by being volleyed it is my own fault'. And again, 'When a fine volley finishes the rally it is as it should be – a weak stroke paying its proper penalty.' In other words, the answer to the man at the net is learn to play better. Thus spoke the two greatest exponents of the competing schools. Mr Renshaw was the finer player of the two, but in logic or prophecy he was inferior to his rival. He had omitted or underrated the limitations imposed by nature on human strength. Volleying from the service line is more exhausting than back play, and the champion himself has been alike in practice and theory compelled to submit to the laws of nature. But Mr Lawford, while advocating in print and enforcing in practice the paramount necessity of strong and accurate back play, had by this time convinced himself that Mr Hartley was right when he said that 'a combination of both styles will always be needed'. About this time, he adopted in part the tactics of his chief opponents. 'He hit as hard as ever to the baseline, but he now followed his stroke close up to the net, and volleyed the return hard across the court'. His long and persistent advocacy in theory and practice of baseline playing received its due reward. He had learned something from the volleyers, but they in turn were forced to resort to his tactics.

A practical equilibrium between the two methods was attained. Since then, the volleying has been as brilliant and unexpected as ever, but it has been not the basis but the result of strategy. The hitting has been harder and more accurate, but it has not been the final end and object of the striker. Each kind of stroke has fallen into its proper place, and the controversy has ceased with the occasion that called it into being. The credit of this desirable consummation should be attributed, as it is due, equally to the Renshaws on the one hand and to Mr Lawford on the other. In the four-handed game, there was much more agreement in principle. Mr W. Renshaw announced, in a letter to the *Field*, his adhesion to the older division of labour. He says, 'the winning game is for one man to stand about the baseline, the other on or just inside the service line.' And Mr Lawford expressed himself to the same effect. This position has now become practically obsolete, and the abandonment of the service line position in the double game was, on the part of the Renshaws, only temporary; but both writers agreed in effect that 'play must be very weak to allow a player at the net to do much good'. Acting on these principles, the old struggle was renewed. The Irish championship was won by Mr E. Renshaw, after a finely contested match with Mr Lawford, in which both games and strokes were almost exactly equal. The same player, in conjunction with his brother, secured also the double championship, and the pair were again successful in the Northern Association tournament, against Messrs Hartley and Richardson.

The championship meeting at Wimbledon was a remarkable one. The two strongest players, Messrs E. Renshaw and Lawford, met in the first round, and the vicissitudes of the match made it one of the most extraordinary contests on record. Mr Renshaw, playing against a violent wind, had a strong lead in the first set, winning five games to one. Mr Lawford then won five games in succession and the set. On crossing over, Mr Lawford only won one game in the second set. In the third, after three games scored to Mr Renshaw, his opponent won a love set. The fourth was a love set to Mr Renshaw, after Mr Lawford had won two games. Changes so sudden and victories so hollow would in any case have made the match memorable, but the end was more singular still. In the fifth set, Mr Lawford won five consecutive games. Then Mr Renshaw in despair tried an underhand twisting service, which, aided by the strong cross wind, drove his antagonist far out of the court. Instead of taking this, as he should have done, backhanded, Mr Lawford tried to crush it forehanded, and he failed, hitting many balls out of court. Aided by fine but somewhat fortunate play, Mr Renshaw crept up game by game, and finally won the set and the match. He afterwards defeated Messrs C. W. Grinstead and Donald Stewart, but failed to wrest the championship from his brother.

As illustrating the relative frequency of the volley at this time, it is interesting to find that in the Renshaw-Lawford match, out of an aggregate of 626 strokes, not including service and return, 502 were taken off the ground, while 124 were volleys, of which Renshaw contributed 97 and Lawford 27; from which it would appear either that the frequency of the volley had been exaggerated, or, as is more likely, that hard hitting and improved placing had already begun to produce their natural effect. In this year, the United States of America, for the first time, sent over two representatives, Messrs C. M. and J. S. Clark, two brothers who, though not claiming to be a representative or champion pair, had not been beaten as a pair in their own country. They played two exhibition matches at Wimbledon against the Renshaws, who were, however, far too strong for them. It was remarked that the up player stood much too near to the net, and was consequently at a disadvantage. Next to the performances that have been mentioned, the principal features of the year were the extraordinary successes of Mr C. W. Grinstead and of Miss M. Watson, to whom Miss M. Langrishe was but slightly inferior, and the first appearance of Miss L. Dod, whose triumphant career will necessitate frequent mention hereafter. Mr Grinstead, in addition to numerous other trophies, was successful at Leicester, Leamington, Exmouth and Brighton, besides beating Mr Richardson at Wimbledon; while in a match at Edgbaston he only allowed his opponent to win a single stroke in a whole set, probably the most decisive victory on record.

The attempt to play by electric light was renewed at Mr Borrie Blair's court near Stockton, one of Dr Siemens' arc-lights, 3,000 candle power, being used. In reference to this attempt, the late Mr O. E. Woodhouse, equally distinguished as a lawn tennis player and electrician, recommended the use of three lights, a large one over the net, covered over, and reflected on a white screen to imitate a ceiling, and also one at each end reflected in a similar manner. It is not known whether the experiment has since been tried; but, should it be repeated, the above suggestion might with advantage be acted upon.

A remarkable innovation on the old method of pairing the competitors in a tournament was also first suggested in this year by Mr R. B. Bagnall Wild. The object was to place all byes in the first round, so that no competitor should sit idle while another is playing a hard match. This was secured by taking the power of two next above the number of entries and deducting from it the number of entries. The difference would be the number of byes in the first round, e.g. with 9 entries, 16 – 9 = 7 byes and 1 match; so, with 21 entries, 32 – 21 = 11 byes and 5 matches, in each case bringing the players in the second round to a power of 2. This system has in principle been universally adopted, and will be again referred to; but it is impossible to pass over altogether an invention so ingenious, the consequences of which have been so remarkable. Such an innovation required time and consideration before it could be generally accepted, and the principal matches of 1884 were arranged on the old system.

1884

The Irish championship was as usual the first in precedence, as it is with one exception in prestige. Mr E. Chatterton, who in the previous year had made a very successful first appearance, was beaten in the final round by Mr Lawford; and the latter had not much difficulty in wresting the championship from Mr E. Renshaw, the holder, who had prejudiced his chance of success by dancing into the small hours of the day of the match. Lawn tennis is an exacting mistress and will not brook dalliance with the attractions of terpsichore. Mr Lawford's game is said to have been of unsurpassed severity, but it should be remembered that it is easy to play a strong game against a tired opponent. In fact, however, he had strengthened his attack since he last met his rival, as was shown at Wimbledon, where Mr E. Renshaw succumbed to Mr Grinstead, who in his turn was unable to do more than win a single set against Mr Lawford. The champion was, however, still too strong for Mr Lawford, who, moreover, was to some extent weakened by an injury to his wrist, and partly perhaps from this cause the play of the champion during the first and second sets was pronounced by many good judges to be the most brilliant that had yet been seen. To win a love set in eleven minutes against a player of Mr Lawford's strength must, at all events, be considered an extraordinary performance, though perhaps too great a drain upon the reserve of physical strength, which, with a view to possible contingencies, the strongest player should always maintain. The interest of the Wimbledon meeting was increased this year by two novelties. A ladies' championship was instituted, which, after a series of interesting matches, was won by Miss M. Watson, who, by this and her victory over Miss M. Langrishe at Dublin, proved herself to be decidedly the strongest lady player. A still more important feature was the transfer of the double championship from Oxford to Wimbledon. The entries for this event had recently dwindled in number and quality; and the Oxford University Club adopted a course not less wise than generous when they resolved to hand their cup over to the All England Club. Stronger entries and a wider interest have in each succeeding year rewarded the self-sacrifice of the donors. A curious instance of the difference between single and double play is afforded by the proportion of volleys to balls taken off the ground in the two respectively. In the single match between Lawford and Grinstead, a persistent volleyer, the volleys were 102, the strokes off the ground 479 – a proportion of 1 to 4¾. In the final match of the double championship, between the Messrs Renshaw and Messrs E. Lewis and E. L. Williams, won easily by the former, the volleys were 314 and the strokes off the ground 156 – a proportion almost exactly of 2 to 1. In extreme contrast to what may be called the condensation of first-class play, where, as between Lawford and Grinstead, there were but one rest of 10 strokes, one of 9, and two of 8, may be mentioned a match at Eastbourne, lasting 2 hours 40 minutes, between Messrs Coote and Avory, in which there was little or no volleying, and one rest extended to 60 strokes. In the second class, the most successful players were Mr Donald Stewart, who won the open singles at Cheltenham and the Northern championship, Mr E. de S. Browne, the champion of the West of England at Bath, Mr E. L. Williams with victories at Leamington and Eastbourne, and, above all, Mr C. W. Grinstead, who, at Chiswick Park, Exmouth, Brighton and Wimbledon, showed that he had no superior except the three great players, who in virtue of their superiority had consistently abstained from participation in local or provincial contests. Messrs R. D. Sears and J. D. Dwight, now so well known in this country, represented America with success at Liverpool and elsewhere. Cambridge for the first time were able with the powerful assistance of Messrs Wilberforce and Lyon to defeat Oxford, which this year had lost the services of Mr Grinstead and depended mainly upon Mr Grove. If the annals of lawn tennis tend to repeat themselves in successive years, one event of 1884 is hardly likely to be often repeated. At Stockton on 5 July a ball in play struck a sparrow very much in earnest and killed it on the spot. This was the last year in which the old system of byes was retained, for at its close, the meeting of representatives recommended and the All England Club adopted Mr Bagnall Wild's scheme with trifling modifications, and thenceforward the absurdity and unfairness of a bye in the later rounds of an important match has been an impossibility. Two minor alterations in the laws were at the same time announced. The first owed its existence to the frequency of foot faults under the old law, and notably in the championship match, when the server was repeatedly penalised for lifting his foot in the act of serving, and the new law 7 now announced was as follows:

> The server shall stand with one foot on the baseline, and the other behind it, no matter whether touching the ground or not.

The law now (1889) reads thus:

> The server shall stand with one foot beyond (i.e. further from the net than) the baseline, and with the other foot upon the baseline.

And an explanation is added by law 9 excluding from the category of faults the lifting of the foot, which is therefore now permitted. Law 17 was also altered so as to provide that

> it is a good return if the ball, having passed outside either post, drop on or within any of the lines that bound the court into which it is returned.

1885

The Hyde Park covered court in Dorchester Square, which took the place of Maida Vale court when the lease of the latter expired, was opened in April 1885 on the occasion of the first Covered Court Championship. Neither of the Renshaws entered, and the title of champion was secured by Mr Lawford, after beating Messrs Donald Stewart, H. Chipp and C. H. A. Ross. Another new championship dates from this year. It was instituted by the managers of the Buxton Tournament under the title of Ladies Double Championship, and has been repeated annually at the same place. The winners on the first occasion were Mrs Watts and Miss Bracewell. The Irish championship was retained by Mr Lawford after a very severe struggle with Mr E. Renshaw. Equally interesting was the match between two younger players, Messrs E. Chatterton and W. J. Hamilton won by the former after an exciting contest. The brothers Renshaw in the doubles, and Miss M. Watson in the ladies' singles, were still superior to their rivals, though against the latter, Miss Martin, with powers of service and volley unusual in a lady, kept the result long in suspense. The All England championship attracted an unprecedented number of spectators. It is said that 3,500 person witnessed the decisive match. Once more Mr W. Renshaw vindicated his title, though with less to spare than in the preceding year. He won three sets to one, but the first and the last were both advantage sets. Mr Lawford resorted to volleying rather more than usual, while Mr Renshaw towards the close was playing mainly from the back of the court, and the result showed that his skill in this department was as conspicuous as in that to which he owed his earlier fame. At a prior stage of the meeting a singular accident had aroused much controversy. A ball struck by Mr E. de S. Browne, which would have dropped in court, came in contact with the foot of the umpire. A decision against the striker was confirmed by the referee on appeal, but the weight of authority failed to secure complete acquiescence. The obvious lesson to be learned from the incident was that the umpire's seat should have been further from the net. Miss M. Watson again proved herself the best lady player, and the Renshaws were still too strong for any other pair. After the three leaders, Mr E. de S. Browne was certainly the most successful player of the year. He placed to his credit the West of England championship at Bath, and the open singles at Cheltenham, and though defeated by Mr E. Renshaw at Dublin and Wimbledon, two games only in the aggregate separate the winner from the loser. Of the rest Mr C. H. A. Ross in the London Athletic Club tournament, Dr Dwight in the Northern, Mr Chatterton at Buxton, Mr E. Lewis at Eastbourne, and Mr Donald Stewart were the most successful, while among ladies Miss L. Dod was steadily working her way to the front. The lists were, however, weakened by the defection of two of the most promising players. Mr Grinstead left England for Canada early in the year, and has been seen no more on our lawns, and the claims of business have allowed Mr E. L. Williams to appear but rarely. Mr Richardson, too, who had been at one time thought not incapable of the highest place, withdrew from first-class play in this year. But lawn tennis players had to mourn a more melancholy loss in Mr Donald Stewart, whose distinguished career was in the month of August closed by an early death, to the deep sorrow of a wide circle of friends.

1886

The season opened in April with the Covered Courts Championship, for which Mr E. L. Williams put in one of his now rare appearances. Both he and his most formidable opponent, Mr Lawford (the holder), were short of practice, but the younger of the two, less affected perhaps by this cause, played extremely well and scored a well-earned victory. The Irish championship was shorn of one of its chief attractions by the non-appearance of the Renshaws. Mr W. J. Hamilton in their absence won the preliminary rounds, but was unable to wrest the championship form the holder, Mr Lawford, who by a third consecutive victory secured the trophy in perpetuity. Miss M. Langrishe beat Miss Martin and won the ladies' prize. Cambridge for the third year in succession won both events in their annual contest, played this year at Hurlingham, against the sister university. At Wimbledon, Mr Lawford, as in the two previous years, vanquished all his opponents, including Messrs Grove, Hamilton, Garvey and Lewis, and won the All Comers prize, but again, as on other occasions, his success stopped there. A crowd hardly less than in 1885 witnessed the struggle for the championship, and they were rewarded by what was, perhaps, the most brilliant performance ever known. Mr Renshaw won the first, a love set, in 9½ minutes, hardly making a mistake, surpassing even himself in the rapidity and versatility of his game, and never giving his opponent a chance. He slackened slightly in the second set, which Mr Lawford, taking advantage of the opportunity, won; but the result of the match was never in doubt, and after a marvellous display of placing, pace and judgement against all Mr Lawford's well-known powers seen at their best, Mr Renshaw secured his sixth championship. Such play had never been seen before; it may be doubted whether it has since been equalled. Miss Bingley created some surprise by her victory obtained by sheer hard hitting and accuracy over Miss M. Watson, the champion of the previous year; but the renewed triumph of the Renshaws in the four-handed match can have caused no astonishment, and was indeed inevitable. Mr E. Renshaw occupied a somewhat less prominent position in this year than heretofore. He was beaten by Mr Lewis at Wimbledon, and by Mr H. Grove for the Northern championship, taking it may be less pains in preparation than some of his rivals. Messrs Browne, Grove and Dwight met each other frequently, and their alternate victories and defeats gave to neither any decided superiority, while Messrs Chatterton, Hamilton and Lewis were little inferior either in merit or success. Among the ladies also a similar equality prevailed. Miss M. Langrishe and Miss Martin at Dublin and Buxton were entitled to equal honours. Miss M. Watson at Exmouth avenged her Wimbledon defeat at the hands of Miss Bingley, while Miss M. Watson and Miss L. Dod could each boast a victory. In effect there was little to choose between the first five ladies, or between the first eight gentlemen, always excepting Mr W. Renshaw, who enjoyed an unquestioned supremacy. The revolution of lawn tennis was accomplished. Its end had been attained, but at this moment it must have appeared probable to many observers that the result had been the establishment of a perpetual dictatorship.

10

The Triumvirate of Lawn Tennis

1887

A great future had, for the last two or three seasons, appeared to be reserved for Mr Lewis, and the expectation of his friends was raised still higher by the easy manner in which, in the Covered Court Championship, he disposed of Mr Williams, the holder. His prospects would have seemed even brighter, could anyone have foreseen the accidents of the immediate future. He was not, however, present at Dublin, and the appraisement of his chance for the championship was necessarily postponed. Mr W. Renshaw was also an absentee, and the array of talent was perhaps less conspicuous than on other occasions. Mr E. Renshaw had little difficulty in the all corners singles, only losing one set – to Mr W. J. Hamilton – in all his matches, and on meeting Mr Lawford for the championship, he won three consecutive sets, and thus recovered the trophy secured by him in 1883. The standard of play on both sides was very high, the first and third sets more than once depending on a single stroke; but Mr Renshaw displayed a steadiness and caution sometimes lacking to his game, and to these qualities he owed his victory. An Irish pair, Messrs W. J. Hamilton and T. S. Campion, won the four-handed championship for their country. But the most distinguished part in the tournament was taken by Miss L. Dod, who only lost one event for which she competed, and who, by successively defeating Miss Martin and Miss M. Watson, assumed the position, which she maintained throughout the year, of the best lady player. The Scottish Championship meeting, held early in June, was rendered important by the fact that Mr W. Renshaw there sustained an injury to his arm, which ultimately compelled him to withdraw from all further participation for the year. This circumstance increased, if possible, the interest of the championship meeting at Wimbledon. If Mr W. Renshaw should find himself unable to play, it was impossible with certainty to select the winner from a list comprising Messrs Lawford, E. Renshaw, Grove, and E. Lewis. Finer play has rarely been seen than that between Renshaw and Lewis, though the former did not lose a set, and displayed to great advantage the same qualities of steadiness and caution that had so much assisted him at Dublin. Mr Lawford was successful after a severe struggle against Mr Grove, and as the champion withdrew from competition, the issue lay between Messrs E. Renshaw and Lawford. The former seemed to have the better chance; not only had he behind him his victory at Dublin, but his play at this meeting had been distinctly superior to that of his rival, over whom he enjoyed the inestimable advantage of ten precious years of youth. Moreover, the older player had had the harder work in the week. All these considerations seemed to point to one result, but conclusive as they seemed, they were fallacious. The early stages of the match were unfavourable to Lawford. He had lost two sets to one and was beginning to tire, and good judges thought his chance hopeless. But Renshaw on this occasion allowed caution to degenerate into timidity, and steadiness into weakness. He allowed his opponent to recover his strength, and with it the fourth set. Then, by the exercise of great determination, and of a physical effort that must have been of extreme severity, Lawford secured at last the coveted title of Champion of England. It was a great achievement. At the age of thirty-six to defeat, in a contest extending over two hours, an opponent ten years younger than himself would have been sufficiently remarkable. But this was not all. Ten times had he entered at Wimbledon, five times he had unsuccessfully contested the championship. He had manfully withstood the prestige of the volley when it was deemed invincible; and single-handed had maintained the value of back play. He had made converts of his chief opponents, and had in turn not disdained to borrow something from them. In each successive year he had learnt something and had gained something. Through disappointment and defeat he had found his way to victory, and he had his reward. It is rare in any department to find so signal an instance of patience and perseverance. The annals of games present no parallel to it.

In the absence of the Renshaws, the doubles were won by the Hon. P. B. Lyon and Mr H. W. Wilberforce, and Miss L. Dod vindicated her supremacy at Wimbledon as at Dublin, Manchester and Bath. As in the previous year, it would be difficult to distinguish between Messrs Grove, E. de S. Browne, Dwight and Lewis, though the number of victories would perhaps award the palm to the latter, while an imperceptible interval only separated Mrs Hillyard – hitherto well known as Miss Bingley – Miss Martin and Miss M. Watson. The remarkable equality that had hitherto distinguished the matches between the rival universities was still maintained, Oxford winning the singles, and Cambridge the double matches.

1888

The idea of a Lawn Tennis Association to embrace all the principal clubs in the country had been before the public for some years. It was not to be expected that the whole lawn tennis world would forever submit to the jurisdiction of a single club, however eminent. But though several abortive attempts had been made in the direction of association in previous years, it was only in 1888 that the idea was realised. Early in the year meetings were held, at which first a provisional and afterwards a definite scheme for constituting such an association were adopted. Rules were framed, the regulations for prize meetings were revised and amended, and an elective governing body was appointed. The council, elected annually, consists of a president, twelve vice-presidents, an honorary secretary, an honorary treasurer, and thirty-six ordinary members. These latter represent six divisions of the United Kingdom, the southern counties returning ten representatives, the northern eight, the midlands six, while Wales and Monmouthshire send two, Scotland four, and Ireland six representatives. The All England Club frankly accepted the altered conditions, and, preceded or followed by all the leading clubs, joined the association, and thereby gracefully abdicated the legislative functions that they had virtually exercised uncontrolled for eleven eventful years. It is too soon to anticipate the consequences of this democratic step, but a young and vigorous body, invested with unlimited power, could not long be expected to discharge merely administrative duties. The composition of the council, which includes nearly all the most prominent players of the day, is the best safeguard against rash and inconsiderate innovation.

Mr E. W. Lewis retained with ease the Covered Court Championship, his assailants being in number and quality alike less formidable than might have been expected. The Irish championship produced a series of matches of the highest interest, the chief feature being the marked advance of Mr W. J. Hamilton since last year. He beat in succession Messrs Campion, Meers, Lewis and Lawford, and was only vanquished by Mr E. Renshaw, the holder, after a most exciting struggle. Mr T. Pim appeared for the first time in this tournament, showing remarkable promise; and of the ladies, Mrs Hillyard, after a very hard fight with Miss M. Langrishe, defeated Miss B. Steedman in the final match. The All England Championship at Wimbledon now seemed a very open question. If the matches at Dublin offered a fair criterion, there could be but little to choose between Messrs E. Renshaw, Lewis, W. J. Hamilton, and Lawford; and in addition to these formidable claimants, Mr W. Renshaw, the champion of so many years, was believed to have recovered from the effects of his accident. Unfortunately, the weather, which interfered so fatally with the tournaments of the year, was not more propitious to Wimbledon than to minor events. The commencement was necessarily postponed, and even after a delay of three days it was found that incessant rain had ruined the courts, and made the results to some extent a matter of chance. A long match on a heavy ground with Mr Grove was not without its effect on Mr W. Renshaw, and on the following day the latter had to submit to defeat at the hands of Mr W. J. Hamilton, whose extraordinary power of rising superior to adverse circumstances was never more conspicuous than on the present occasion. On subsequent days, both the weather and the ground improved, and though soft and devoid of life, the lawn was not altogether unfit for play. Mr E. Renshaw, on two successive days, beat Messrs Hamilton and Lewis, in neither case without a severe struggle, and by defeating Mr Lawford, the holder, secured his first championship. The new champion had fairly earned his title : with the exception of his brother, he had himself met and vanquished all the best players in the list of entries, and though at no time was the ground in good condition, it must yet be remembered that in a variable climate the weather is not the least formidable of the antagonists with whom a player has to reckon, and taking the prevailing conditions into account, Mr Renshaw played throughout a sound and at times brilliant game. The Messrs Renshaw, playing through from the commencement, won the four-handed championship, and Miss L. Dod maintained against Mrs Hillyard the position she had gained in the previous year.

The meeting had taken place under new auspices. Mr J. Marshall, who had so long been the honourary secretary of the All England Club, had resigned his office, and Mr H. W. Wilberforce had assumed the burden of management. As might be imagined from their fine performances at Wimbledon, Messrs Hamilton and Lewis swept the board at the minor meetings. Among the trophies of the former were the Northern and Welsh championships at Liverpool and Penarth respectively, while Mr Lewis careered from London to Leicester, from Chiswick Park to Exmouth, and where he came he conquered. Mr E. Renshaw displayed extraordinary skill in giving successfully the most crushing odds, and among other interesting specimens of his powers in this department he gave Miss L. Dod at Exmouth the odds of thirty, and at Penarth conceded to Mrs Hillyard half forty – tremendous odds considering the strength of the recipients – and he won upon each occasion.

Bad weather caused the abandonment of the Oxford and Cambridge matches, so that the balance still remained equal between the two universities. All England Championships are necessarily limited in number. Absolute exhaustion of the supply had not, however, yet been reached, and the managers of the Northern Tournament embraced the opportunity. They instituted what is probably the last of the series under the title of 'All England mixed doubles championship', which was won by Mr E. Renshaw and Mrs Hillyard.

1889

The entries for the Covered Court Championship have never been as numerous as might have been expected from the interest of the contest. Commencing in 1885 with nine competitors, it attracted a similar number in the next year, ten in 1887, six only in 1888. while in the year under review, three competitors only presented themselves. Mr Lewis had no difficulty in retaining his title, but unless the interest in these matches can be revived, it may be feared that a competition, attractive in itself, and rendered more so by the fact that it is unique, is doomed to extinction. New covered courts having now been built and opened at the Queen's Club, Kensington, it is possible that this branch of the game may receive a new impulse.

Irishmen have the right to contemplate with entire satisfaction the result of the championship meeting at Dublin. Never since the year of its institution had they succeeded in retaining their own prize. But this was their hour of triumph. Mr W. J. Hamilton defeated the Renshaws on two successive days, and at last, after ten years of eager expectation, an Irishman was once again champion of Ireland. His success was as well deserved as it was popular, and gave promise of an even greater victory hereafter.

In the doubles, the Messrs Renshaw were forced to resign their position into the hands of Messrs Lewis and Hillyard, and in the ladies' competitions, Miss L. Martin, and her partner in the doubles, Miss Stannell, reaped the chief honours.

Twenty-four competitors entered for the All England Championship. In the list were comprised almost all the most eminent players of the day. Two only were missing, and both were Irishmen – Messrs H. S. Mahoney and J. Pim were unable to compete. The success of Mr Hamilton at Dublin might well encourage his countrymen to hope that for once the tables might be turned, and that an Irishman might at last bring back from Wimbledon the coveted honour of which they had not had hopes so fair since the days of Mr V. Goold. But their hopes were again disappointed. Their champion did indeed beat Mr Lewis, but to the general surprise, Mr H. S. Barlow, after a closely contested five-set match in which he seemed for a long time to be decidedly at a disadvantage, defeated Mr Hamilton. The next day a still closer and more remarkable struggle took place between Messrs W. Renshaw and Barlow. The latter won two sets and held an advantage in the third. Mr Renshaw saved himself with difficulty, winning the set by the narrowest margin after his opponent had been within two strokes of the match. Again Mr Barlow took a strong lead. The score was called five games to two in his favour, and he was four times within one stroke of victory, but his opponent again made a decisive effort, and though repeatedly in imminent danger, ultimately won the set, after no less than eighteen games had been played. He had no sooner done so than he once more allowed his game to go to pieces, and Mr Barlow won five consecutive games. Then at last the old champion woke up, and 'playing grandly, and winning game after game amidst tremendous excitement, brought the score to games all', and thus caused a fourth advantage set to be played. He then won the deciding set and the match. This year had produced many sensational matches, in the course of which fortune had repeatedly transferred from one side to the other her uncertain honours; but in none of them had the turns been so sudden or the denouement so tragic. It was certain, at all events, that Mr Barlow had at a bound made good his claim to a position in the first class of players. Mr W. Renshaw played far more steadily against his brother for the championship, and winning with comparative ease resumed the place he had held so long as the first of lawn tennis players. Thus, just as in the first three years of the championship, it had passed from hand to hand, so now in these last three years, the three greatest exponents of the game had each scored a victory.

The Renshaws avenged the defeat they had sustained at Dublin by winning the doubles against Messrs Lewis and Hillyard, and in the absence of Miss L. Dod, Mrs Hillyard once more occupied the position that she had held once before in 1886 as Miss Bingley. In the last set of the deciding match, Miss L. Rice's score was at five games to three and 40–15, so that the interest of this match also was enhanced by an unexpected revulsion. Next to Messrs Hamilton and Barlow must be classed Mr Lewis, who at Chiswick, Exmouth, Teignmouth, and elsewhere, repeated his triumphal progress of last year. To Mr Hamilton, however, must be awarded a nominal precedence, the Irish, Welsh, and Northern championships having all fallen to his share. In the final match of a handicap at Howth, he was called upon to owe fifty, and in addition to give fifteen and a bisque to a fairly good player.

The score was several times called 40–owe 50, so that to have a chance of winning the game he had necessarily to win seven strokes running, a feat that he performed on more than one occasion, and eventually won the match. Among the ladies besides the winner of the championship, Miss L. Rice, Miss Jacks, the Misses Steedman, Miss Martin and Miss Stannell, and Miss L. Dod have been highly successful; and the two universities are still unable to claim any superiority one over the other, Oxford having won the single and Cambridge the double match.

There remains to be recorded yet another interesting feature of the year. The Lawn Tennis Association had instituted an inter-club challenge competition, for which they had framed a code of rules. England, Wales, Scotland and Ireland are divided into eight divisions, each division being subdivided by counties or other areas. The matches are to be played in three stages; the first between clubs in their respective subdivisions, until one club only be left in each. The winner of the first stage has then to compete with the winners in other subdivisions, until one club be left in each division. Finally, the eight winning clubs in the eight divisions contest with each other the third stage of the competition. The preliminary processes having been gone through, the last stage took place at the Queen's Club, when the All England Club defeated the Whitehouse L. T. C. after a close contest. An inter-county competition had also been instituted under the same auspices. Middlesex and Surrey were left in to play the final matches, which took place at Exmouth, and the Middlesex team proved successful by the odd event only. An audacious innovation introduced at Scarborough may not be passed over in silence. Two competitions took place there entitled, respectively, Veteran Ladies' Singles and Veteran Mixed Doubles. The courage of the handicappers deserves admiration no less than the candour of the competitors; and the love of lawn tennis must indeed be deeply implanted in the female breast, if the craving for odds can vanquish a reluctance that has been the despair of census enumerators, and which even in courts of justice the most solemn sanction has frequently been powerless to overcome.

The supreme legislative powers with which the Association was invested in 1888 have not long been allowed to remain in abeyance.

In January 1890, important alterations of the laws were introduced. The change of sides, instead of being at the end of each game, is to be made at the 'end of the first, third, and every subsequent alternate game of the set', and 'the winner of the toss may, if he prefer it, require the other player to make the first choice'. As a result, the service will no longer come from the same side throughout the set, and the anomalous disadvantage of winning the toss ceases to exist. A more important change, which is, however, not compulsory, was made in the method of handicapping players. Bisques, which had been borrowed from tennis, are abolished, and instead of the alternating odds of half fifteen, half thirty, etc., which without the aid of bisques would be too widely separated from the next integral point of odds, smaller fractional parts – viz. one-quarter, two-quarters, and three-quarters of fifteen – are introduced, which may be given or owed in augmentation of other odds. One-quarter of fifteen is a stroke given at the beginning of the second, sixth, tenth, etc., games; two-quarters of fifteen is a stroke given in the second, fourth, sixth, games; three-quarters of fifteen is a stroke given in the second, third, fourth and sixth, seventh and eighth games, and so on. The change was dictated mainly by hostility to bisques, which have never been popular with lawn tennis players, partly because they do not possess a constant value, still more perhaps from the mental effort required to employ them discreetly. Yet it may be doubted whether the substitution of fifteen and two-quarters of fifteen for its equivalent of half-thirty will conduce to simplicity; and the already overburdened umpire will in the case of owed odds find that an additional demand is made upon his capacity for mental arithmetic, while a more serious defect, arising from the undue prolongation of matches in which heavy odds are owed, is left untouched. Nevertheless, it may be hoped that the difficulty will not be found insuperable, and that all lawn tennis players will in the interest of uniformity loyally accept a change made by competent authority on weighty grounds and after due consideration.

Such is the history of lawn tennis and so great has been its progress. Its condition today is as flourishing as the warmest enthusiast could desire. No one can dispute the immense advance that has taken place in the average quality of the play. It is shown by the great increase in the number of players of the second and third class. In a large number of counties a local championship now exists, and the local champion is in almost every case a strong and often a brilliant player. The proficients of both sexes are counted by thousands, where ten years ago they would have been limited to tens. But this is not all. Much as the average merit of the 'masses' has increased, that of the 'classes' may be said to have increased in an equal ratio. Three players at least must now be included in the first class, in addition to those other three to whom a monopoly has so long been conceded. And the second class press closely on the heels of the first. To the list of those who have been so often mentioned in these pages that they do not need repetition, must be added a host of names so great indeed that many who with justice might be included must necessarily be omitted. Messrs Goodbody, J. Baldwin, A. G. Ziffo, P. and G. E. Brown, G. W. Hillyard, H. Chipp, E. G. Meers, C. G. Eames, J. C. Kay, C. L. Sweet, T. S. Campion, and W. Baddeley. To all these and to many more a distinguished career is assured, or may be confidently predicted.

To attempt to anticipate the future would serve no useful purpose. There are many styles and many diversities of play. The method of the Renshaws is not that of Lawford, and Hamilton, Barlow and Lewis differ equally from them and from each other. Whether the game of the future will be a development or modification of one of these styles, or whether some new departure is in store for us, is beyond our power to foretell; but the success of Major Wingfield's experiment is no longer a matter for conjecture or doubt. Poets and moralists have loved to trace the growth of great results from small beginnings, but they might seek in vain for an illustration of an origin so humble, a progress so rapid, a development so vast. Not in this country only, but wherever the English tongue is spoken, lawn tennis has taken firm root. Boulogne, Brussels, Cannes, and Homburg are but specimens of the Continental towns that have fallen victim to the prevailing infatuation. Before 1881, it had overleaped the Atlantic, and from that date the championship of the United States has been an annual event. From Antigua and Melbourne, from Natal and Singapore, in India and China, in Pernambuco and Victoria, the results of matches are regularly reported. Nor is the extent of its diffusion more remarkable than the number and variety of its worshippers. Introduced avowedly as an amusement suitable to both sexes and to every age, it has more than fulfilled the expectations formed of it. Not only to the vigorous athlete, but to the child, the girl, the middle-aged man immersed in business, and to the man of grey hairs, it has served as a health-giving yet not too absorbing pastime. The favour with which it is regarded has apparently increased with every year. Pessimists may discover, to their own satisfaction, symptoms of a waning popularity, but these are imperceptible to unprejudiced observers. The germs of decay may lurk in it, as they do in the youngest and most vigorous forms of life, but they are as yet undeveloped, and at present it would be difficult to predict from what source is hereafter to come 'the change, the check, the fall', unless, indeed, it arise among lawn tennis players themselves from a conflict of irreconcilable claims, or from a disloyalty to the pursuit they profess. Lawn tennis is in danger neither from external attack nor from natural decay; its prospects are assured, if only it be true to itself. Not even in the case of cricket and football are the great matches watched by larger crowds with keener attention or a more intelligent appreciation. The names of the great players are 'familiar in our mouths as household words'. The distinguishing features of their play are known and understood by hundreds of persons who never take part themselves in the game. That the Wimbledon championship has escaped the demoralising influences that have turned the university and public school cricket matches into vast undiscriminating picnics is an fortunate circumstance, both as inspiring hope for the future and as attesting the inherent vitality of the game. Few spectators attend from fashion or indolence, nearly every visitor to the ground is drawn thither by a living and personal interest, and what is true of Wimbledon is true of Dublin, Liverpool, Edinburgh, and countless other lawn tennis centres, where the performances of 'the favourite' are watched with an excitement not less eager and far more disinterested than at Epsom or Newmarket. The annalist of lawn tennis, at least in this its hour of triumph may be permitted to give expression to a confident belief that the day is far distant when a future writer will be called upon to narrate the gradual stages of its Decline and Fall.

11

The Court

Were a millionaire to advertise for a perfect lawn tennis court, it is likely enough that he would be able to expend money up to any assigned limit, but it is not by any means certain that he would obtain what he desires; and any competent and fairly honest person to whom he might apply, even if given *carte blanche* as to expense, would probably decline the task. A perfect lawn tennis ground is, in truth, a rare and precious possession. There are certain indispensable conditions that will not indeed secure a perfect ground, but without which not even a tolerable one can be produced; and these conditions, though in theory easily attainable, are precisely those that in practice are found most rarely to exist. In the first place, the lawn must be level. It must not be on a hill either in length or breadth, nor may it resemble a hog's back, sloping from the centre to the sides, or from the net to the baselines. It must be of sufficient size to admit of an ample margin all round – that is to say, there must be a space of not less than 21ft from the baselines, nor less than 12ft from the sidelines, to the limit of the ground. Yet it should not be unlimited: too vast an area makes it difficult to measure the strength of the stroke, and to see the ball satisfactorily. A background of shrubs is for the latter purpose the pleasantest to the eye, and this is generally possible on private lawns; but on club grounds, a background of nets is in most cases the best that can be hoped for. Where a background of shrubs exists, these must be entirely subsidiary to lawn tennis, and no inherent beauty can be allowed to interfere with their single purpose. If a shrub in its natural growth encroaches on the prescribed space, were it the loveliest and most unique specimen in the kingdom, it must be removed or curtailed as ruthlessly as though it were the meanest plantain. No shrub or tree that can by any possibility cast a chequered shadow upon the court at any time of day can be allowed to exist, though a court entirely in deep shadow is pleasant enough.

The ground must lie lengthways from north to south, otherwise 'the low sun lends the colour' in a sense that, however attractive to poet or painter, is destructive of good lawn tennis. From some perversity of nature or art, this condition, though of primary importance, is generally wanting, while many of the others are often wilfully ignored. The quality of the soil is rarely a matter of choice, but where possible it should be remembered that natural is better than artificial drainage.

Due consideration having been given to all these conditions, the selected ground must next be prepared for use. Where natural drainage does not exist, the land must first be thoroughly drained by means of a 3-inch main drain running along one side of the court, and 2-inch spur drains discharging into the main drain at an angle so as to impede as little as possible the flow of the water. It is very important to do this some time before proceeding to sow or turf the surface, because the trenches cannot be filled in so firmly as to prevent the ground from sinking afterwards. The drains should not be covered in until they have been proved to discharge the water freely. The extent of the drainage will depend on the quality of the soil; but as it is far better to have a ground too dry than too wet, it is well to err at all events on the safe side. On heavy clay land, the drains should be 30in. deep, and not more than 5 yards apart, and even then the ground will probably be improved by the addition of a thin layer of chalk, fine rubbish, or cinders, placed on the clay below the surface soil. Lighter lands will not require this additional expense, and the number of the drains may be slightly reduced. The whole ground must next be carefully levelled. For this nothing is required but a number of wooden pegs, string and a spirit level, with the addition of a gardener who understands his business; but if the process of levelling requires soil to be brought from a distance, and the soil so brought is not all of the same kind, a layer of each kind should be placed over the whole plot, putting the retentive material at the bottom, and reserving the finer and more friable portions for the top. The necessity for this arises from the preference for certain soils shown by particular grasses. The added mould will very likely be full of weed seeds; it is therefore very advantageous to burn it, especially if it be of a clayey character. When the surface is perfectly level and absolutely smooth, the top soil may be replaced, after which the rake and roller should be diligently used to secure a fine, friable surface. At this stage in the preparation of the ground, a cheap and easy method of providing sitting accommodation for a large number of spectators, available where the ground prior to levelling was on a slope, may be resorted to. It has been adopted by the Earl of Cavan, whose grass courts at Wheathampstead, Herts, may be said to approach very closely to perfection. The bank bounding the court is cut into the shape of an armchair with a sloping back. Such a bank will be naturally dry, and the damp can when necessary be effectually excluded by cushions or rugs. If the court is required to be used at an early date, and economy is not a special object, turf is to be recommended in preference to sown grass, and for this purpose down turf is the best of all possible kinds if it can be procured in the neighbourhood; but it must be remembered that, however closely the turves be laid down, they are apt to separate under a hot sun or drying wind, which will cause ugly seams to disfigure the entire surface, and for this reason, in most cases, and especially if early use is not insisted on, sown grass is to be preferred. Before sowing, the quality of the soil should be improved by a free use either of well-rotted stable, farm or artificial manure. Where the latter is preferred, 2 cwt of superphosphate of lime, 1 cwt of Peruvian guano, and 1 cwt of bone dust mixed together are recommended by Messrs Sutton – whom there can be no better authority on the subject – as an excellent dressing sufficient for an acre of ground. About ten days after the application of the dressing, the seedbed is ready for sowing. The best time for sowing is from the middle of March to the first week of May, and from the middle of August to the end of September, or even later. Seed may be sown liberally in autumn, and the process repeated in March, and the court may then not improbably be fit for a moderate amount of play in the following summer. In a favourable season, the present writer has found this to be so, but such a result cannot always be counted on. It is of great importance not to stint the seed on the score of expense.

The amount should never be less than 75lbs per acre, or 1lb to every two rods or perches of land, while a still more liberal expenditure of seed will be repaid by the more rapid clothing of the ground, and the more closely the plants are crowded, the finer will be the herbage. The seed will be more evenly distributed by two sowings than by one, the second crossing the first at right angles. A still day should be chosen, and the sower should keep his hand low, as grass seeds are very light and easily blown away. After sowing, the entire surface should be raked in order to cover the seeds, and then rolled twice all over. The depredation of birds is most easily prevented by a number of lengths of twine with strips of glittering tin suspended at intervals so as to turn freely in the wind.

The description of seed to be used will depend on the nature and quality of the soil, and it will generally be wise on this head to consult one of the great seed merchants, such as Messrs Sutton or Messrs Carter, who have made it a subject of scientific experiment. For the present purpose, it will be sufficient to indicate a few of the best grasses for ordinary soils without specifying the proportions in which they should be mixed, a matter that will be better learned from an expert. Clovers should be avoided, as they do not wear well and hold the rain; they should, therefore, be used only where the soil is peculiarly liable to be scorched in summer. The best grasses for lawn tennis grounds are crested dogstail (*Cynosuruscristatus*), sheep's fescue (*Festuca ovina*), hard fescue (*Festuca duriuscula*), fiorin (*Agrostis stolonifera*), several descriptions of meadow grass (*Poa pratensis*, *Poa trivialis*, and *Poa nemoralis sempervirens*). Crested dogstail is peculiarly adapted to dry loams or a chalky subsoil, sheep's fescue to a sandy or rocky soil, while the meadow grasses are better suited to the stronger and moister qualities of land. The best mixtures will consist mainly of the above varieties, and should be obtained from some first-rate seedsman in preference to resorting to local dealers. The percentage of germination of even the best seeds varies greatly, increasing from 60 or 65 per cent in the case of fiorin, to 90 or 95 per cent in sheep's fescue, but from old seeds such as are frequently supplied by inferior dealers, the percentage of germination is likely to be so small as to cause the labour and expense of sowing to be almost entirely wasted. Most of the best seedsmen give a guarantee both of purity of seed and of percentage of germination, by demanding that the purchaser will escape much of the risk of failure. He should, however, be careful to specify the purpose for which the seed is intended, many mixtures admirably suited to ordinary lawns being quite inappropriate for our purpose. In most old lawns, clover will be found in large quantities, but as it will make the ground slow, the amount, if excessive, should be reduced by the application of nitrogenous manures. Rye grasses as a rule cannot be recommended, but perhaps an exception may be made in favour of a dwarf small-seeded variety of perennial rye grass, such as *Lolium peremte Suttoni*, which receives a high character as a quick-growing, close, fine and hardy plant.

As soon as the young plant is high enough to be topped, the scythe may be resorted to, as being at first better than the mowing machine; but afterwards the latter should be constantly in use, never while grass is growing at all less than once a week, and in moist warm weather nearly every day, and at all events often enough to prevent the sward from ever looking ragged. Worms have a beneficial action on the soil, which is good for the grasses; but during the summer worm casts are a great annoyance, and on newly sown lawns infested by worms they often prevent the germination of the seeds by loosening the soil to excess. Lime water, which is perfectly innocuous to grass, if sprinkled over it, causes the worms to come to the surface, where they can be easily removed.

With every precaution, annual weeds are sure to appear, and these can be held in check by constant mowing; but the more formidable weeds, plantains, thistles and dandelions must be cut out with a knife one by one about an inch below the surface, care being taken to remove as much of the root as possible. A plantain cut off just below the collar will send out a number of shoots, and the process of extirpation must be repeated until by successive attacks the plants have been so weakened that the grasses can assert their superiority in the battle of life. This is naturally a slow and somewhat tedious process, and if a quicker result is desired, a drop of vitriol upon the cut root will if carefully administered have a speedier operation, attended, however, with the risk of causing bare places in the turf. Constant use of a court will keep down daisies, as they do not bear being trampled on; but on private lawns where there is not much play, nitrogenous manure will assist the grasses to overcome the daisies. Where moss is prevalent, it is caused either by dampness or by poverty of soil, and should be remedied by attention to the drainage or by the application of manure. When the turf becomes worn in particular places, a very small change in the court will relieve the pressure on the worn spot and enable the grass to grow again; at the end of the season all the patches should be re-sown, and a dressing of the artificial manure recommended above, or of about half a hundredweight of Norwegian fish guano, applied to each court. Road scrapings are useful for the same purpose. Before re-sowing, the ground should be vigorously raked, and a little fine earth should be sifted over the seed, and the whole rolled twice in different directions. Under no circumstances should the grass be allowed to seed, a course that only weakens the plant and does not materially thicken the growth. Where the soil is not so heavy that trampling will be injurious, it will be much improved by folding sheep on it for a month or two in autumn or winter. The sheep should be fed with a little oilcake in addition to hay or roots. This is generally done on club grounds, but is hardly possible where the lawn forms part of the garden. In such a case where play is suspended for a time owing to the absence of the family from home or any similar cause, it will be found useful to mow the grass constantly, leaving all the cut grass on the ground, and if this be done additional manure will in some cases hardly be necessary.

In conclusion, it must be repeated that a good ground is essential to good play. To make such a ground requires some amount of expense, and to maintain it will entail a good deal of trouble. The chief points to be firmly kept in view are constant mowing and rolling, change of the lines of the court as soon as it shows signs of wear, frequent examination to see that weeds shall never get the upper hand, and occasional restoration to the plant of those constituent elements that it requires as food. But the initial expense and the trouble of maintenance will be amply repaid by the drier and firmer surface, the absence of weeds, and the elimination of false bounds.

12

Hard Courts & Covered Courts

In many parts of the world, lawn tennis players can find no turf to play on. In England there is abundance of excellent turf, but it is available only for a few short summer months, and not always in these. It is not surprising, therefore, that from the first introduction of the game, a substitute for grass has been eagerly demanded. We might, perhaps, wonder that the substitute that can be used for so great a portion of the year when play on grass is impossible, has not long ago driven its prototype out of the field, and that this has not been the case is no small tribute to the merits of turf, though it is due partly to the charm of out-of-doors play, partly to considerations of economy, still more perhaps to the defects of all substitutes hitherto introduced. If, for instance, our climate admitted of the formation and maintenance of the excellent sand courts used at Cannes, and elsewhere on the Continent, it may be doubted whether the popularity of the turf could have remained unimpaired, but, as matters stand, it appears that grass, during such time as it is fit for play, is in no danger of serious competition. Its principal rivals out-of-doors have hitherto been gravel, concrete, asphalt and many combinations of material differing from, but partaking more or less of the characteristics of, the two latter materials. To these must now be added brick dust courts, which may possibly be destined to a wide sphere of utility. Gravel courts, though at first sight attractive, have many serious defects. They must be very carefully constructed, and require much attention to keep them in order. With the utmost care a very slight frost, followed by a bright sunny day, renders them quite useless. They are of a bad colour, and are ruinous to shoes and balls alike. With these drawbacks they are not very likely to be extensively patronised in the future.

Concrete and cement are open to many objections. They are fatiguing to the eyes and limbs, and trying to the feet; the surface is generally so rough as to be destructive of balls and shoes alike; and, in addition to this, it is liable to crack with frost. Cinder courts have never enjoyed much popularity, and are not extensively in use at the present time. They are cheap and easy to construct, but the surface is so gritty, and balls are so quickly blackened and worn out by contact with it, that it does not seem necessary to say much of this material. Asphalt courts are expensive, and liable to crack under the influence of frost, and to be affected by a hot sun. They are also apt to be too smooth for safety or for a satisfactory bound of the ball, and change of temperature not unfrequently causes them to sweat. Nevertheless, asphalt is probably the best of the materials above mentioned for use in England in the winter, and can hardly cost more than some at least of the alternatives that have at various times been proposed or tried. So long ago as 1881, a basalt court was constructed in Australia, and two years later it was described in the columns of *Pastime* as being altogether satisfactory. It is not known to the writer whether any court has been constructed in England on the same principle. After levelling the ground, lay first a layer of broken blue stone, 2 in. gauge; then a layer of broken blue stone, 1 in. gauge. All the material placed on this must be passed through boiling tar before being used, and should consist as follows:

1. Of a layer of broken blue stone, ⅝ in. gauge.
2. Of a layer of the same, ⅜ in. gauge.
3. Of a layer of the same, ³⁄₁₆ in. gauge.

A heavy roller should be constantly passed over all this during the operations. The whole thickness of these layers amounted to 4½ to 5 in., of which the last but one should be ¾ in. thick, and the last a little less. A coating of the finest blue stone dust must then be spread, and the floor left for a week, after which time liquid tar must be poured upon it from cans with rose spouts, and this should be swept all over the surface in a thin film with ordinary stable brooms, blue stone dust being again spread over it to absorb the surplus tar, which is sure to 'sweat out' from time to time. This system costs but 2*s* 6*d* per square yard in Australia. Blue stone is the name given there to basalt.

A stone flagging round the floor is said to be advisable, as being convenient to work to, and the floor should be left at least a fortnight before playing on it. It is stated to have stood two years' use under the full blaze of an Australian sun without deterioration. The cost of such a court 40 yards long by 21 yards wide in Australia would at the price given have been about 105*l*; but the contractor said that he would not put down another such floor under 2*s* 9*d* or 3*s* per square yard. It was stated that the same basalt could be bought in England at 15*s* or 16*s* a ton. The cost of this material would of itself be likely to deter imitators. A cheaper material, for what may conveniently be called a 'brick rubble court', was proposed by a correspondent to the *Field*, writing from Beckenham, a year or two later, to be constructed in the following manner:

1. Level to 12 in. below the proposed surface, and consolidate with rams.

2. Trench for a 3 in. land drain pipe round the court, and for six rows of 2 in. pipes across it at equal distances apart; the pipes to lie on an impervious clay bottom 3 or 4 inches below the top of the trench and packed in rubble up to the level of the foundation bed. Secure sufficient fall and a good outfall.

3. Cover the foundation bed with 4 in. of large brick rubble, and ram it down.

4. Spread 4 in. of coarse ballast (burnt clay) sifted of its finer portion by a ¼ in. riddle, and roll well.

5. On the top of this roll in a layer 2 in. of finer ballast, i.e. ¼ in. stuff sifted by a ⅛ in. riddle. Consolidate this layer with water, and do not spare the roller.

6. The remaining 2 in. of bed are to be a mixture of burnt Thames sand, and the finest siftings of ballast, in the proportion of four or five of the former to one of the latter, mixed by riddling through a ⅛ in. sieve. Roll lightly.

7. Lay on the final layer 1 in. above the intended level, and roll down to that level with free use of water and with a heavy roller. The cost is said to be 60*l* to 70*l*, and it is stated (1889) that time has only improved the court, and that, the material having sunk to the proper level, the yearly cost of maintenance is very trifling. Every autumn the surface is raised, re-levelled, and rolled; and in this way all worn places are repaired and green mould eliminated, while the drainage is improved.

About the same time another correspondent, residing at Sutton, wrote to the same journal recommending a much cheaper court, which, being laid on chalk, required no drainage except a fall of 8 in. from side to side, the area being 105ft by 56ft. The ground having been levelled to a depth of 8 in., forty loads of burnt brick rubbish at 3*s* 6*d* a load about one-quarter of a brick in size were laid down on the surface, carefully raked and levelled, and then other twenty loads of rather finer material were added. This was rolled one day with a horse-roller, and again for two days with a hand-roller, after which it was well rammed all over. Fifteen loads of the refuse sifted as fine as possible were then added, rammed well, and rolled with a hand-roller for three or four days. The writer is assured by the gentleman who constructed this court that the fall from side to side was barely perceptible, and might be dispensed with on a chalk foundation, the natural drainage being perfect. On a clay subsoil, a few drain pipes would be required, involving an additional outlay of 4*l* or 5*l*. When first laid down, this court cut up a little, and required raking and rolling after play; but after three or four months, the surface consolidated perfectly, and required nothing more to be done to it. The total expense of this court barely amounted to 20*l*, and it may certainly be pronounced to be as economical a lawn tennis court as could be desired, or as has ever been constructed. It must, however, be borne in mind that from the nature of the subsoil, no drainage was required, and that the material was obtained within three-quarters of a mile. On a heavy soil, and where the material must be brought from a distance, the cost would be proportionally increased. Like the court last described, it shares with gravel the defect of suffering from thaw after a night's frost; but no open-air court can in this climate be entirely free from this drawback.

Brick dust – A very useful winter court, known as the 'brick dust' court, has been for some years in use. Several of these have been constructed by Mr E. Randall, builder, of Claygate, near Esher, who has kindly furnished details of the method of formation. After excavating to a depth of about 6 inches, the ground is made perfectly level and even, after which 3 or 4 inches of coarse brick rubbish is placed upon it; the surface is levelled, the rubbish is further broken up, and the whole 'punnered' or rammed down to a fairly even surface. Kiln dust, taken from under the burned clamps of bricks, is next procured from the brickyard and screened through a ⅜ in. screen. The coarser portion, which will not pass through the screen, is then laid down evenly and well rolled and rammed, after which the finer portion of the brick dust is put on with a rake and well rolled. The amount of material required for a court 120ft by 60ft would be about sixty loads of the coarser kind, and forty loads of the finer. This kind of court appears to require little care to keep it in order, and receives high praise from those who have tried it. The cost varies from 30*l* to 50*l* according to the distance and expense of procuring and casting the materials. If constructed in the winter, the ordinary rainfall will be sufficient to consolidate the surface, but in summer some amount of watering will be desirable. No raking, but rolling only, is required to keep it in order; but it should not be used during the progress of a thaw. When the frost is out of the ground, it should be rolled. The best way to mark out this court is to apply fresh-slacked lime with a whitewash brush, repeating the process on a new court three times. The court should be surrounded by a wire netting 6ft or more high to keep the balls in. If they become wet from contact with the grass or ground outside the court, the brick dust adheres to them; in no other way does the material appear to cause any inconvenience, and wind is said to have no effect upon the court. Of course, it is affected by alternate frost and thaw in the same way as most of those previously mentioned; but, after making all deductions, many good judges consider the 'brick dust' court the best that has yet been invented for winter use, while the cost is very moderate and the trouble of maintenance trifling.

A short description may be here added of a court recently made at the Hotel d'Albion, Hyeres, in the south of France, though it cannot be recommended for imitation in this country, the climate of which is hardly suitable to a court so slightly constructed. Ten inches of soil having been excavated, about 6 inches of rough stone direct from the quarry are packed as closely together and as evenly as possible, and a thin layer of gravel, or even earth, is placed on this to fill up all interstices. Upon this is placed a mixture of lime, sand, and refuse from the gasworks, thoroughly beaten and rolled down. The refuse is introduced to prevent the growth of weeds, for which purpose a solution of sulphate of copper would be equally effective. After all, these courts, though available on many days in winter, are often, at least in England, rendered useless by the state of the weather, and the player who is desirous of practising throughout the year, irrespective of rain, snow or frost, must have recourse to a covered court.

The number of these is already considerable, and may be expected to increase in proportion to the increasing number of players who, by the facilities already afforded to them, have seen and appreciated the singular beauty and interest, as well as the scientific character, of this branch of the game. Those who, by this means, can play lawn tennis throughout the year, have an immense advantage over those of their rivals whose practice is limited to the short and capricious duration of an English summer. It is conceived, therefore, that no apology is necessary for going at some length into this question. Many private owners and clubs have erected covered courts that are admirable in many respects, approaching more or less nearly to excellence in proportion as their builders have been guided by the lessons that experience has taught. The essentials are, of course, an ample margin round the court; a good floor, in regard both to substance and quality; abundance of light without glare; adequate ventilation without uncomfortable draughts; and sufficient height to admit of the game being played on similar conditions to those found out of doors in regard to lobbing. Spacious galleries and dressing rooms are accessories that, though not indispensable, are hardly less important to the comfort of players and spectators. Of the above conditions, some of the older courts are deficient, particularly in the matter of margin, height, lighting and ventilation. Avoiding, however, any invidious insistence upon these defects, it is proposed here to describe with some minuteness one court that, by the unanimous opinion of those who have been privileged to make use of it, is the most perfect that can be found at the present time. This court belongs to the Earl of Cavan, is situated at Wheathampstead in Hertfordshire, and was completed in 1888. It was erected by Mr F. Owen, Gustard Wood, Wheathampstead, under the personal superintendence of Lord Cavan. For the floor, 16 in. of clay were first cut away, and on the surface so made 12 in. of cement concrete were laid down. Above that, 6 in. of a composition in which a specially prepared gravel, cement and three or four other ingredients are combined, and which was the outcome of repeated experiments conducted by Lord Cavan and Mr Owen. This composition is practically indestructible, is rougher and firmer, and not more costly than asphalt, and is believed to be superior to that material in the bound of the ball; at all events, those who have played on the court have been unable to find any fault with it in this respect. It is stained a very dark brown, approaching close to black. The total area of the floor is 124ft by 63ft, so that the margin outside the court is from each baseline to the wall 23ft, and from each sideline 13ft 6 in., an interval ample enough to satisfy the demands of the most active player or of the most exacting critic. The court is constructed with cast-iron stanchions, wrought-iron girders, principals, and Louvre, cast-iron ornamental cresting, with galvanized-iron sides, the plates of which overlap in order to prevent the entry of wet, and ends to the following dimensions: 124ft long, centre to centre of end stanchions; 67ft 6 in. wide, centre to centre of stanchions; 22ft high at the eaves; 38ft high to the under side of the ridge of the roof; the lowest tie rod is 27ft from the ground, but in the centre of the court, for a distance of 40ft, the lowest tie rods are raised to a height of 30ft by the introduction of four columns and girders placed near the net, two on each side. A height of 30ft at the point where the ball must reach its greatest altitude thus secures to the most inveterate lobber ample scope for the exercise of his talent; but if this is not enough, as the tie rods are round iron bars only 2 in. in diameter, any ball missing them is considered in play, so that there are eight additional feet of height in which a lobbed ball may conceivably disport itself. In fact, however, few balls surmount the tie rods. The whole of the roof is glazed with ⅜ in. 'cast-plate glass', on Helliwell's patent system, without the use of wooden sash bars, so that the maximum of light is obtained, while the glare of the sun is obviated by a solution of whiting, size and glue, two coatings of which will last through the six winter months. The iron sash bars are constructed in such a manner that the moisture caused by condensation is carried away by a small water channel, which discharges into the eaves gutter. All the work is painted black inside and dark green outside. The Louvre ventilators are fixed on both sides of the lantern light in the roof, and run the whole length of the building. To prevent penetration by snow, they have movable shutters, covered with very fine perforated zinc, but these shutters can be left open if desired. A platform runs the whole length of the lantern, which admits of easy access. There are two side galleries, one opposite each net post, approached separately from the outside, to prevent any obstruction to the players. One of these is enclosed for warmth, fitted with a stove, filter, etc, and is used as a tea room. Each has a dressing room at one end. At one end of the court is a building, partly intended as a gallery, from which to watch the game, while the rest is used as a lavatory, fitted with cupboards for rackets, etc. In addition to the Louvre ventilators, there are sliding 'hit and miss' ventilators in the iron sheets of the walls, and eight of the sheets are made to open bodily. All floors composed of asphalt, or of the composition used at Wheathampstead, are liable to sweat when temperature changes suddenly; so far as possible this is here obviated by the use of two of Doulton's radiating stoves, and one mail-clad stove, by Petter of Yeovil, the pipes of which are carried up inside the building, and stoves and pipes are protected by wire guards. It is needless to say that the erection of such a court as is here described has necessitated a large outlay. The total cost was 2,400*l*, of which the galleries, house and heating apparatus are responsible for about 400*l*. Expenditure might be reduced by diminishing the area of the floor and the height of the court, but the sacrifice of efficiency would be great in proportion to the saving effected.

It must not be supposed that the choice of material for the floor is limited to asphalt or cognate substances. In the opinion of many of the best judges, a well-laid wooden floor is the most suitable to covered courts. It has two advantages over what may conveniently be called 'metal' floors. One is the absence of jar to the feet, which, on asphalt, is considerable, especially to players of middle age, and the second is the closer resemblance of the bound of the ball to that which is obtained from hard and lively turf. The disadvantages are the greater expense and the difficulty of keeping boards perfectly even without frequent 'trimming' or re-planing. The floor of the old Maida Vale court, now demolished, was of asphalt, and is still highly spoken of by all who played upon it; but the Hyde Park Club court, which in 1885 replaced that at Maida Vale, was constructed with a wooden floor, which is, however, not considered altogether satisfactory. It occupies an important position as the scene of the Covered Courts Championship, which, since the institution of the Hyde Park Club, has been played there annually. It is 106ft long by 49ft 6 in. wide, giving a margin of 14ft at each end and of 6ft 9 in. from the sidelines of the double court to the wall. The glass roof has a span of 54ft, and the lowest obstruction to the ball is a girder, which, in the middle of the court, is 23ft, and at the sides 20ft, above the floor. In the three essentials of height, space and lighting there is little room for complaint; but the floor is composed of parallel wooden boards about 4 in. wide, laid on bearers 1ft apart, and fastened in such a manner that no nails appear on the surface. It is said that boards so laid have a tendency to separate and work up when played on, so that they frequently require trimming, and also that the bound of the ball when it drops over a joist is not the same as when it pitches between two joists. The boards should not be less than 1¼ in. thick, and 1½ in. would be better. For some reason much practice is required to familiarize a player with the peculiarities of this floor, and to this cause may partly be due the comparative indifference with which this interesting championship has been lately regarded.

It is probably with a view to avoid these defects that the fine new courts at the Queen's Club, West Kensington, opened in April 1889, have been constructed on a different principle. The two courts are side by side in one building, with pillars between them, on which rest respectively the two roofs, forming a double gable. There is a margin at the sides of each court of 10ft, and an interval between the two, therefore, of 20ft. The two parts of the building being of unequal length, there is a margin at each end of one court of 20ft, and of 17ft at each end of the other. It is lighted by side windows as well as from the roof, the glazed space in each roof being about one-fourth of the whole area; but, as each court contributes light to the other, the total amount is greater than if the buildings had been separate. The height of the spring of the roof 23ft from the floor, and that of the tie rods in the centre, which form the lowest obstacle, is 28ft 6 in. The floor is composed of rectangular blocks of wood, 11 in. by 2⅞ in. and 1½ in. deep, laid herringbone fashion, and known as Duffy's patent woodblock flooring, each block being pinned to its neighbour. With the view of making the floor rather less solid than it would otherwise be, these are laid on felt nearly half an inch in thickness, the whole being placed on a layer of cement four inches in depth. The whole of the floor is alike, and the bound and pace of the ball are said to be as near as possible the same as on a hard grass court. One of the courts has recently been taken up and relaid, and is described as being excellent in all respects. The floor and walls are coloured dark green, as being more cheerful than black, and the inside of the roof is painted white.

The covered court erected at Creaton, near Northampton, by Mr F. N. Langham, can hardly, in strictness, be called a lawn tennis court, as all the walls are there brought into the play. Owing to the facts that the court is smaller than the normal size, that the ball may be taken off the walls, and that the service line is placed at 23ft from the net, practice in this court is of little use for the usual game on grass; but it is so pretty and interesting in itself, and the cost of erection was so small, that a short account of it is here given. The dimensions are 70ft by 33ft, with a height of 23ft. The side walls are of wood, and are 8ft in height, above which the ball is out of play. The whole of one end wall, and so much of the other as is below the spectators' gallery, is in play. It is lighted by windows in the side, 5ft 6 in. high, and above these springs the corrugated-iron roof. The cost of the whole building only amounted to 439*l*, of which the floor, composed of the best French asphalt, cost 102*l*, the roof representing 137*l*, and the timber and labour about 200*l*. The windows, having been given, are not included in this calculation, and the wood was obtained from the Cottesbrooke estate at a slightly reduced expense. After taking all these circumstances into consideration, it is probable that the price of a similar court built by contract would be 480*l* to 500*l*. Mr Langham also considers that the court would be improved by the addition of 4 feet to its length, and that lights ought to have been introduced into the roof; two alterations that would have added slightly to the initial expense. In any case, the Creaton court is probably the cheapest, and not by any means the worst, thing of its kind, though it must be admitted that, if the game played in it can be described as lawn tennis at all, it is at least a specimen of a somewhat original type.

If a comparison can usefully be instituted between the relative fastness of these various materials with that of grass, it may be said generally that the bound of the ball, even on lively turf, is the lowest and slowest. A wooden floor is slightly faster than grass; the composition used at Wheathampstead is a little faster than wood, and asphalt heads the list in this respect, though, being smoother, the rise of the ball is perhaps a little less on asphalt than on the other materials. A comparison of this kind, however, cannot be strictly accurate, for the liveliness of grass varies so greatly from differences soil and of thickness of heritage, that it is very far from conforming to a fixed standard. Suggestions have been made to counteract what has been sometimes considered the excess of bound on the harder courts by a corresponding change in the ball; it is believed, however, that players find little difficulty in adapting themselves to varying conditions of floor, and that the maintenance of uniformity in the standard ball is a matter of much higher importance than any advantage that might be secured by a uniform ratio between the quickness of the floor and the bound of the ball.

13

The Implements of Lawn Tennis

It is hoped that readers who have taken the trouble to peruse the previous two chapters will now be prepared to make the large assumption that the ground has been levelled and turfed in the most approved manner, as well as manured if necessary, that all bare patches have been re-sown, that the grass has been most carefully mown throughout the early spring, and constantly rolled whenever the weather has made it possible or desirable, and finally that all weeds have been scrupulously eradicated. If the gardener has been induced to do all this, and has performed his duty conscientiously, the enthusiastic lawn tennis players of the family will pronounce him an inestimable treasure, and will willingly condone any shortcoming in the produce of the vinery or the appearance of the flower garden. Even club grounds, where vineries do not exist and flower-beds are superfluous, will probably be found to require frequent visits and constant supervision on the part of the secretary, if he does not wish to be disappointed by the condition of the ground at the commencement of the season; but on private lawns the owner, or at least a member of his family, will on cross-examination be generally compelled to admit that much of the rolling and weeding at all events has been due to his own energy and perseverance.

If in a previous year he has not been satisfied with implements in use, he will have taken care to replace them during the winter with more serviceable articles; otherwise the advent of May will find the manufacturer's time so fully occupied that it will be impossible without vexatious delay to obtain what is required in sufficient quantity or of the necessary quality. The first in order of use, though not in importance, of these implements is the lawn tennis marker. Of these there are many varieties, all no doubt answering their purpose in a fairly satisfactory manner. The relative merit of these, as of all other implements noticed in this work, is a matter of opinion, which in order to be of any value should be based on experiment. Any higher authority than this the present writer does not wish to claim in reference to this or any other implement used in the game, but of the markers he has seen or employed one of the most serviceable is the 'Caxton', patented and sold by Mr F. H. Ayres. It is in use at many of the principal clubs, is simple and does not easily get out of order, and moreover is not so addicted as some other varieties to the fatal vice of splashing. There are two qualities of the 'Caxton', the best as usual being also the most expensive, and it is represented in the woodcut.

It is worked with a chain, which is more effective and trustworthy than the cogwheels used in the cheaper pattern, and it is also furnished with a handle by which the shoot conveying the whiting to the marking wheel is dropped on the tank wheel. The shoot is represented in the engraving as in actual use. The marking wheel is 1⅝in. in width, and the rim of the tank is turned over expressly to prevent splashing – a result that is more important to secure because some umpires and most players are apt to pronounce a ball in court if they have seen the whiting fly. Another excellent marker, even simpler in construction, is sold by Messrs Slazenger & Sons, and is called by them the 'Waterfall'. The principle is that of the common waterwheel, raising the whiting to a platform, whence it is discharged upon a marking wheel 1½in. in width; and the advantage claimed for this method is that grass, dirt and other extraneous matters are completely excluded from the tank.

The best and easiest way to secure a rectangular court is to use a square, but this is not always procurable, and in its absence the following methods may be recommended. For the four-handed court, having roughly ascertained its limits, fix the position of the net, and from the point immediately under it where one sideline is to be measure 39ft From the corresponding point where the other sideline is to be measure 53ft ¾in.; one angle of the court will be where these two lines intersect each other. Ascertain the other angles in a similar manner, and connect all the angles by means of the marker. Then measure 21ft on each sideline on both sides of the net, and 4ft 6in. on the baselines from each corner of the court, put in pegs and connect them with string. The points of intersection of the strings will be the angles of the service courts, and the connection of these points of intersection will give the service lines and service sidelines. Next bisect the service lines and connect the points of bisection, and the double court will be complete. The single court may be marked in the same way, except that the diagonals from the net to the corners will be 47ft 5¼in., and there are of course no service sidelines. Where the same area is intended to serve for the single and double courts, the service sidelines of the double court must be prolonged to the baselines to form the sidelines of the single court.

For the purpose of service, the central point of the baselines should be clearly indicated.

The court having been thus marked out, the posts next require consideration. The chief requisites of a good post are, first, that it shall keep its position in any ground in all weathers; and, secondly, that no portion of it, introduced either for ornament or as part of the mechanism, shall be allowed to project above the prescribed height of the net. This limitation absolutely excludes from consideration a large number of the posts that may still be seen in use. The handsomest and on the whole the best yet produced are the 'Cavendish' posts, and in ordinary soils these keep their position in a manner that leaves little to be desired. Each rests on an iron foot, which on the outer side is secured by two T iron spikes, or feather pins, about 2ft long, which are driven into the ground up to the head at an angle of about 45°. The copper wire rope supporting the net passes over the top, and is then attached to a wheel inserted in the post, easily worked by a handle at the side and checked by a ratchet. If the soil is very light, it maybe necessary to increase the length of the T spikes, or in such case it may be better to adopt a different method of attachment, which is stated to be adequate to the task of keeping the post upright, even in sand. This is called the 'Championship' lawn tennis post, for which a screw is employed instead of spikes. For this, a 'driver' is required to make a hole in the ground; a screw 2ft long is driven in with a spanner nearly to the level of the soil; the foot of the post is then inserted under the head of the screw, and a very slight turn of the spanner suffices to make and keep everything firm. The wheel and ratchet arrangement is the same as in the 'Cavendish' post.

Both of these posts are rather expensive, and, being made of ash wood, if not removed from the ground at night or in wet weather, their lower portions are apt in time to rot from the damp. To obviate these two objections, but especially that of expense, a new post has recently been introduced, which is called the 'Cyprus'. It is constructed of iron, and being tubular, is lighter and less unwieldy than most posts of that material. The foot and spikes to secure it are on the same principle as in the 'Cavendish' post, and the wheel and ratchet winder do not materially differ from it, while the price is considerably less. It may be advisable to increase the size of the foot, which has a tendency to bury itself in soft ground, and so to draw the post out of the perpendicular. All the above implements are made and sold by Mr Ayres.

Mr Gardiner's 'Club' post also is excellent. It rests in a socket and is removable at will. The socket is furnished with a plate fixed at right angles to the direction of the net, the great leverage of which makes it capable of withatanding almost any strain. Mr Slazenger's 'Association' lawn tennis pole is somewhat similar, but to increase its stability, a second smaller plate is added lower down, facing outwards. A flange at the top of the socket is designed to prevent it from sinking too far into the ground, while to avoid the trouble of passing the copper wire of the net through the winder, a chain is fastened to the latter fitted with a bar. The loop of the wire is passed over the bar, and wire and chain are then wound together on the winder. Gardiner's and Slazenger's posts share the advantage that the lawn can be mown without disturbing the sockets, while they are open to the objection that considerable force must be exerted to fix them, and a rather large hole is made in the ground. It is not to be supposed that these are the only posts in existence that are fairly satisfactory. Many others might be mentioned, the best of which are but little inferior to those named above, while the worst of them are far superior to any system requiring the support of guys or ropes. Perhaps it is not too much to hope, as the price of some of the best of the self-supporting posts has been brought to so low a figure, that we have now seen the last of the old rotten rope attached at the one end to a post dragged far out of the perpendicular, and therefore of a quite incorrect height, and at the other to a peg that the tension has drawn out of the soil, and that every five minutes requires the application of a not unfrequently ineffective mallet.

Good nets may be procured from all the well-known dealers. They should be tarred and waterproof, and it is the truest economy to get them of the best quality. If properly taken care of these, will last a very long while, the only necessary precaution being to remove them from the posts every evening. If this is not done, no net, however good, can be expected to last long; nor can any post, however carefully constructed and fixed, keep its position permanently in any soil It would seem unnecessary to insist on this self-evident proposition, did not experience prove that on private grounds removal is the exception and not the rule. On many club grounds not only the nets, but the posts also, are removed after use, to their great advantage in respect of durability and consequent economy. The top of the net should be bound with a strip of white canvas about two inches broad, without which most players find it difficult to see the top of the net, especially when the light is bad.

Many ingenious devices have been adopted to ascertain and secure the proper height of the net. The simplest is a stick or iron fork; but each of these methods is open to the objection that the ball frequently strikes it and is deflected from its course. The use of a chain is not liable to this defect, but it has been found to wear out the net, and cannot, therefore, be altogether recommended. The least objectionable form of chain is Slazenger's net regulator. The centre of the prong is sunk in the ground so that the lawn tennis marker can pass over it, and the chain is attached to a leather loop passed round the edging of the net. The chain, of course, neither expands nor contracts, and the inventor claims for the regulator the advantage that no part of the court is concealed by it. On the whole, the neatest appliance yet produced is Hope's 'Pattern' band, fitted with an adjuster, i.e. a straining screw, to counteract the rise or fall of the net from increased or diminished moisture. The band being made of canvas is, of course, liable to contract in damp weather, and further experience of the counterbalancing screw may perhaps be required before it can be unhesitatingly recommended.

One essential to good lawn tennis – the most important of all – has yet to be mentioned. It is needless to say that this is the ball, and in theory at least, no one will be found to deny that, if lawn tennis is worth playing at all, the best balls in the best condition should always be employed. The time has gone by for insisting on this particular in respect to public tournaments, but at many private or semi-private meetings, competitors are still expected to play with old, worn, dirty and flabby balls, while it is a commonplace occurrence on private lawns to find these, and even a worse sample, supplied without hesitation or apology. It would be equally unnecessary to insist at the present time on the fact that, unless intended for some special purpose, balls must be covered with white cloth, were it not that complete sets of lawn tennis implements, advertised and doubtless sold, still sometimes include a certain number of uncovered balls. All good balls now in use are under-sewn – a vast improvement introduced by Mr Ayres – the result of which has been that whereas formerly the stitches would give way before the ball had lost its elasticity, the covering will now in almost all cases outlast the ball itself. In general it is of little use to attempt to keep balls through the winter. A trial may be made with occasional success in a dry, warm cupboard; and not only frost, but even a moderate degree of cold, as well as damp, must be carefully avoided. It might be worthwhile to add the precaution of keeping balls in sawdust to exclude the air, but with the most elaborate care they will generally be found after the winter to be dead and inelastic. Good balls are sold by many makers, conforming in size and weight with the requirements of the laws; but so long as Ayres' 'Championship' balls are, as is now the case, selected for use at nearly all the chief public tournaments, it is unnecessary, and would be useless, to mention other descriptions.

There is far more scope for individual taste in the selection of a racket. The essential points are: a good hoop, free from knots, with a well-marked and continuous grain; a plain wooden handle, round or slightly octagonal, fitting the hand of the player, and attached to the middle piece without any perceptible interval; and good strong gut. The screw that passes through the hoop and the middle piece is important, and should be carefully examined. The thickness of the hoop is to some extent a matter of taste. The thinner hoop has rather more 'play', but far less durability; while a very thick one will probably be found to be too tightly strung, and certainly will increase the weight of the racket. In any case, there should be sufficient strength at the 'bow', just below the centrepiece. It is possible to string too tightly, though this is a defect that a few days' play will generally modify, and the degree of tightness desirable varies with the style and taste of the player. The racket, when swung lightly by the butt, must come easily, yet not too easily, and good balance is not to be tested altogether by the centre of gravity or by any other rule. An experienced player will know what suits him better than anyone else can tell him, and will soon become accustomed to any slight divergence from theoretical perfection, while a beginner will seldom be able to choose a racket for himself, and had better resort to some competent adviser. The weight is an equally important matter, and to a still greater extent depends on the style of the player. Within limits, weight means increased power, and lightness greater resource. Taking, therefore, 15 oz. as the maximum and 14¼ oz. as the minimum to be recommended, there is considerable room for choice. A volleyer by preference will generally select a lighter racket, and the habitual back player one approaching to the maximum weight; but each description of player may take as a guide the rule that, while it is an advantage to use a racket as heavy as is compatible with absolute freedom, there should, nevertheless, always be a margin for possible emergencies and sudden effort. The shape of the racket is of less consequence. The curve, borrowed from tennis, which was so marked a feature in the type in vogue a few years ago, was valuable so long as most strokes were made with a horizontal racket. Now that most hard strokes are made with a racket nearly vertical, the curve has become less desirable, or even injurious, as tending to increase the difficulty of striking the ball with the middle of the racket. The Messrs Renshaw prefer to have a slight curve, while Mr Lawford brings the curve to an irreducible minimum. The illustration on page 115 is from a racket made in 1889 for the writer by Tate, who has been for many years racket maker in ordinary to the three distinguished players above mentioned, as well as to many more of the best-known players of the day. Among makers of less expensive rackets of excellent quality may be mentioned Holden, Ayres, and Slazenger, the last of whom has introduced a slight additional curve, technically known as a 'lob', on the lower side of the head of his rackets, for the purpose of adding to the weight of that part. This innovation is believed to have been suggested by Mr E. W. Lewis, and to be approved by many first-class players as giving increased force and severity both to service and drive.

Players should at all times have at least two pairs of shoes – one for use when the grass is in the smallest degree damp, with a leather sole fitted with the short nails known as steel points, which are allowed on all grounds, though spikes, screws and other nails are prohibited; the other pair for dry grounds, with either a roughened or smooth India rubber sole. Those who play much on asphalt frequently feel the unpleasant jar to the feet caused by so hard and unyielding a substance. A special shoe has been introduced by Messrs Cording, consisting of an ordinary India rubber sole, above which is a layer of spongy India rubber covered over with a thin strip of leather. The result is said to be a high degree of durability and elasticity combined. With these remarks, intended as an expression of opinion only, the whole question of dress may safely be left to individual discretion.

Such are the implements without which lawn tennis cannot conveniently be played. Among those which, though not necessary, are useful, may be mentioned the racket press to keep the racket from warping and losing its shape. To a player who uses a light racket, this is essential, unless he be one of those epicures who buys a new one every year. The writer has one of Tate's rackets, which has stood the wear and tear of eight seasons and the ordeal of restringing, and, though it has never been in a press, it has not lost its shape or warped in the slightest degree. Such a piece of wood cannot, however, be counted on by a purchaser. Two flat boards of sufficient thickness to keep them from warping, with one or more screws, are all that are required, and the cost of the simpler kinds is very moderate.

Wherever matches are to be played, an umpire's chair becomes necessary. A few years ago, a fragile chair unstably balanced on a rickety table was considered good enough, and the accurate scoring of the game was not facilitated by the discomfort of the situation. It may have been partly for this reason that secretaries and managers have found it so difficult to procure an adequate supply of efficient umpires. The only requisites are sufficient height and stability. These are fairly realised by Hope's 'Pattern' umpire's chair, which is furnished with a back, the inclination of which might easily be made capable of being varied at will, and a small desk to hold the scoring card.

A perfectly satisfactory scoring board has not yet been produced. It is, of course, not generally required on private lawns, so that the ingenuity of inventors has not been stimulated by a large demand. It is an article that can hardly be made beautiful, so that the aim to be attained is limited to facility of manipulation and clearness of expression. The names of the players, and the number of sets, and of games in the pending set already won by each, must be denoted. Numerical figures require mechanism, and unless carefully used are apt to give an erroneous record. It is for this reason, as well as on the ground of expense, that a scoring board known as the 'Abacus', because it follows the principle of the old game of that name, is on the whole preferable. White and black wooden balls are strung on a wire at the side of the words 'Sets' and 'Games' respectively; and one of the balls is pushed forward into prominence from behind the board by means of a stick at the conclusion of a game or set. No mechanism is required, and the balls are easily seen from most parts of the ground.

It is believed that the preceding list includes all implements either necessary or useful to the game of lawn tennis. It may still be necessary to add that in tournaments, each court should be separated from those adjoining it by high nets, and that on private lawns players will find comfort for themselves, economy of balls, and the retention of temper, all promoted by the free use of common nets, which may be procured almost anywhere at the price of twopence per running yard 6ft high. A nominal height of 9ft would be better still, as the nets lose considerably in height as they are drawn out in length. When they begin to wear out they may be handed over to the gardener, to serve the meaner use of protecting next year's strawberry beds. The youth of dirty balls may be renewed by the ball-cleaning machines sold for that purpose by J. Osmond, or by the cheaper and simpler agency of the hall door mat, and the same means will remove green grass stains; but soaked balls are of no use for any purpose, and it is but lost labour to bestow any pains upon them. For this reason they cannot be washed with much success, and all attempts to restore whiteness to balls by 'trouncing' or otherwise have been found useless, and have been practically abandoned.

14

On Umpires

A cynic has summed up the case for and against the sex that comprises more than one half of the human race, by remarking that it is 'impossible to live with them, or to do without them'. Something of the same kind might be said with less discourtesy and at least equal truth of umpires at lawn tennis. It is one of the weakest points of the game that, not only is it impossible to do without them, but that so many are required. The fourth recommendation appended to the 'Regulations for the Management of Prize Meetings' runs thus:

> In important matches, it is desirable to have seven line umpires in addition to the scoring umpire – namely, one for each baseline, one for each service line, one for the half court line, and one for each sideline.

Eight umpires for one match! The referee may well consider that this consideration alone will prevent his lot from being a happy one. Other games make no such demands on the unselfishness of their votaries. At cricket two umpires, or, including the scorers, three or four, are all that are allowed. Tennis, rackets, football, billiards, are even less exacting in their requisitions, though in all of them there is a large professional class who may be, and generally are, pressed into the service, while in lawn tennis, for the present, no such class exists. In its absence, players and referee alike are compelled to put up with what they can get, and to make the best of it. It is impossible even to say that any one of the eight is really superfluous, though, from the necessity of the case, many of them must frequently be dispensed with. The scoring umpire will find that the further sideline is almost impossible to judge correctly from his seat, and the baselines come next to it in difficulty, the task of watching simultaneously the foot of the server and the service line being especially hard; so that three line umpires would appear to be almost, if not quite, essential to accurate marking. It is well pointed out by Dr Dwight, that the

> umpire is an unfortunate necessity, and his first object should be to make himself as little conspicuous as possible, and to annoy the players as little as he can.

The duties of umpires and the mode in which they are to keep the score are defined at length in the 'Regulations for the Management of Lawn Tennis Prize Meetings', and it would be tedious to discuss them in detail. Only a few general principles may here be laid down for their guidance. The most important is a thorough knowledge of the laws and of the regulations generally, as well as of the conditions of the particular match, without which no umpire can perform his function satisfactorily. He must ascertain that the net is at the right height before the commencement of play, and measure and adjust the net during play, if asked to do so, or if, in his opinion, its height has altered; but few things are more annoying to players than unnecessary interruptions for this purpose. He should say nothing whatever unless an appeal is made to him, until the ball has dropped out of court, and in that case, the moment it has touched the ground, he should call 'Out!' loudly and distinctly, so that the players may be sure to hear him. When he has a reasonable doubt, let him direct the players to 'play it out', and at the conclusion of the rest he can either ask the opinion of the line umpire or decide the point himself. But if the question be really one for his own judgment, he will generally act wisely if he give his verdict at once. The decision of the moment will in most cases be right, while any attempt to argue the matter out in his own mind will only tend to confuse him. He should follow the ball with his eye the whole time, and with the greatest attention, instead of watching the line. If he adopt the latter course it will often be extremely difficult for him to judge on which side of the line the ball has dropped. He should not allow himself to be influenced by the fact that the player, being uncertain whether the ball will drop in or out of court, has taken it at the half volley. The writer once had to play two long and quite unnecessary sets because, in the arrogance of the moment, he returned at the half volley a ball that dropped out of court, and in fact determined the match in his favour, but which the umpire naturally concluded to be in play because it was returned. Whatever he does, let him under no circumstances appeal to the bystanders. If he do so, he will probably get two prejudiced opinions, both – if such a thing be possible – wrong; and if, when he has given a decision, he should hear, as he certainly will, the outspoken comments of the crowd, he should be as though he heard them not. He should enforce the rules strictly, and send for the referee at once whenever any question of law arise. It is not the duty of an umpire to point out reasons for his decision, unless he be asked a definite question. There is even in that case nothing in the laws or regulations to compel him to do so, but it is conceived that he may legitimately, after calling a fault, on being asked the reason, explain that the service was delivered from the wrong court, or that the server's foot was not on the line, though no direct authority to do so is given him. There is certainly nothing requiring or authorising him to volunteer the information.

In the four-handed game, on the contrary, if a player serve out of his turn the umpire is expressly ordered 'as soon as the mistake is discovered by himself or by one of the players, to direct the player to serve who ought to have served'. The law is silent as to whether he ought to interfere if he sees that a mistake of this kind is about to be made, but the wording of the law, by casting upon him the initiative, lends some probability to the belief that he is intended to prevent as well as to rectify an error. It would appear, further, that a service delivered by the wrong partner ought to count as a fault, but there is nothing in the laws to make it so. A rest played out and any fault served before discovery of the mistake is to be reckoned, and the contingency of the completion of a game is provided for, but it is clearly the duty of the umpire to interfere if possible before a stroke can be scored. Upon all other points, the laws and regulations are sufficiently explicit, and the difficulties of umpiring relate, not to principles, but to the manner of applying them. The task is often a very arduous one, and players and spectators alike ought to endeavour to avoid every unnecessary addition to its difficulty. They should remember that in respect to discretion, the umpire is exceptionally well placed for a view. He has been specially selected for the office and must be presumed to have an adequate knowledge of its duties. He is perched on a high if rather rickety seat, with nothing, except sometimes the player himself, intervening between him and the ball, and with nothing to divert his attention from it. In respect to competence, therefore, he should be invariably treated as capable of giving a sound decision. Most of the spectators, on the other hand, are singularly ill-placed for observing the ball, and their attention is constantly drawn away by other claims, such as conversation, dress or other matches going on simultaneously; and though the players themselves can judge certain doubtful balls accurately enough, there are others on which they will be the first to admit that they can offer no certain opinion.

In respect of interest, the umpire has a still greater advantage. Not to speak of the players themselves, whose relation to each other and to the score is such as to make an absolutely impartial attitude almost impossible, it must be remembered that the spectators are very frequently husbands, wives, brothers, sisters or friends of the competitors, and that they occasionally increase the strength of their natural by the artificial stimulus of a bet. Umpires, on the other hand, do not bet, and ought, *prima facie*, to be credited with absolute impartiality.

In respect both to discretion and interest, it follows that, when there is a difference of opinion between the umpire and a player or spectator, the benefit of the doubt should be given to the former, and it is not in accordance with the best traditions of the game for an aggrieved competitor to stride up to the umpire and, brandishing the racket in his face, to demand in a stentorian voice whether he is ever going to decide a stroke rightly. Nor, when an umpire has had the misfortune to disagree with each player in turn, does it assist him in the performance of his duty to hear one of them mutter angrily to the other as he flings the balls across, 'Well! It is all right. That's one to each of us.' Nor again, when the umpire on appeal has pronounced 'Play', is a little knot of spectators justified in murmuring, not in an undertone,

'Six inches over the line'. Yet these are no imaginary instances, but have been actually witnessed at public lawn tennis matches, while less aggravated specimens of a similar tendency, though admitting of much excuse, are frequent, and must contribute in a marked degree to the notorious difficulty of obtaining umpires. It should always be remembered, also, that an umpire intends to do his best, that he has generally assumed his present position against his will, and only on repeated solicitation, and that he would much prefer the comfortable seclusion of the stand to the dangerous dignity of the scorer's seat; and, after making all these allowances for his shortcomings, it will be well, in the plenitude of Christian charity, to add yet one more, and to recollect, even when he has decided the stroke against you, that he is still a fellow-creature entitled to so much consideration as is due to the fact that, after all, he is there for your pleasure and not for his own.

15

Handicapping

The soothsayer who spoke these words to Antony must have had a low estimate of the handicappers of his day; and though too polite to attribute the result to anything but 'natural luck', he held the opinion that with the most accurate adjustment of odds the better man has always something in hand. This is certainly true of lawn tennis. The stronger player, unless crushed by excess of odds, has always a reserve in service, skill, judgment and confidence that will probably suffice in a close contest to turn the scale. Still, handicaps are so useful and so attractive that they now form an essential element in every important tournament save two. The duties of the handicapper are difficult and delicate in a high degree, and the precise method in which they are to be performed is a matter of pure discretion, often exercised upon insufficient information. Every year, however, the number of 'classed' players grows, and with regard to these the difficulty decreases, while in other cases the adjustment of odds is often merely conjectural. The principle of handicapping is an old one, and was first put in a practical shape in reference to lawn tennis by Mr Henry Jones in a letter to the *Field*, under date 7 July 1883. The bisque, now abolished, was the unit, and all the possible degrees of merit were indicated by classes separated each from the other by one bisque. Since the substitution of quarters of fifteen for bisques, quarters must be taken as the unit, but the general principle will be the same. The regulations provide a series of classes of odds given and owed; in each case Class 0 is scratch, and Classes 1–12 receive or owe respectively the odds of one-quarter, two-quarters, etc., up to forty. Even this is not the limit of possible owed odds; for in 1889, Mr W. J. Hamilton was required to owe fifty in addition to odds given. These classes are divided each from the next by one quarter, and are assumed to correspond with every possible quality of play. The handicapper has to distribute the competitors over these classes as equitably as public form, private information or blank ignorance will allow; but when judging of the unknown, he may fairly bear in mind that, before a handicap, players not unfrequently profess a more modest estimate of their capacity than on other occasions. Into the exercise of the handicapper's discretion, so far as relates to classing the competitors, it would be rash to intrude. Discretion is an autocrat and will not submit to dictation. The regulations direct that 'when the difference between the best and worst players is great (say more than thirty), it is desirable to handicap the best players at owed odds'. The first point is to ascertain the best player and put him at scratch; then the second best, and handicap him with the best. Next find the worst player; if he would not require more than thirty, the handicap may be made from the best player; but, should he need more, then the second, third or fourth best may be placed at scratch, and the handicap made from him, those superior to him being required to owe what is necessary, and the inferior players receiving as many quarters of fifteen as correspond with the class in which they are placed. A player owing odds is required to win one or more strokes in each game, or, in the case of fractional odds, one stroke in the prescribed games, before his score reaches love; e.g. a player owing one-quarter of fifteen must win a stroke in the first and every subsequent fourth game of a set before he can reach love, while the same odds when received are given in the second and every subsequent fourth game. The object of this is to prevent, wherever it is possible, the concurrence in the same game of odds given and owed, and to distribute them more evenly through the set. It will be seen by reference to the Regulations that a player at scratch gives to those below him precisely so many quarters of fifteen as there are classes between them. When the odds received by either player are small, the classes below scratch will meet at the difference between their respective odds; thus Class 2 (receiving two-quarters) will give to Class 6 (receiving fifteen and two-quarters) the odds of fifteen; but where greater odds are given a different principle is observed; e.g. Class 2 will give to Class 12 (receiving forty) not the difference between their respective odds, which would be thirty and two-quarters, but thirty and three-quarters. The reason is that two players, each in receipt of odds from scratch, do not start at the odds they receive, but the superior player starts at scratch; thus, if a player in Class 4 meets one in Class 8, they do not start at fifteen-thirty, but at love-fifteen. But the odds are calculated from the hypothetical scratch man, and as the game is longer than it would be if they started at fifteen-thirty, the better player has more opportunity in which to display his superiority. He is required, therefore, to concede one quarter more, and the terms on which these players actually meet are fifteen and one-quarter – these are called differential odds. A similar analogy is followed when two players meet who are both above scratch. Taking the same example as before, if players in Class 4 (owing fifteen) and Class 8 (owing thirty) are drawn together, the former will start at scratch. The game will then be shorter than if they started at owe thirty to owe fifteen, and by the application of the differential principle the superior player owes to his opponent not fifteen, but one-quarter less, viz. three-quarters of fifteen. No such interference with the relation between classes is necessary where a player owing odds meets one who receives them, and these will start, therefore, at the positions they respectively occupy on the handicap list. In classing the entries, it should not be supposed that the value of a stroke owed corresponds precisely with that of one received. The difference must be to some extent conjectural, but it will perhaps be safe in practice to put the ower as against the receiver of fifteen one class higher than that in which he would be placed if the values were equivalent.

In four-handed matches, the task is more difficult. The strength of a pair must generally be very uncertain, but a basis at least can be obtained by first classing each player individually. The strength of any pair will be their united odds from scratch (expressed in quarters of fifteen) divided by two. If the strength so estimated is expressed by an uneven number, one-quarter must be added before dividing by two, and pairs will meet at the difference of their respective odds with the addition (or, if both pairs owe odds, the subtraction) of differential odds when the table requires them. Thus, if A, owing fifteen, and B, receiving fifteen and one-quarter, being partners, meet C, receiving fifteen and two-quarters, and D, receiving thirty and three-quarters, to ascertain the strength of A B, deduct the odds owed by A from those received by B. Add one-quarter to make an even number, divide by two, and the odds received by the pair from scratch will be one-quarter. Next add together the odds received by C and D, add one-quarter to make an even number, divide by two, and the pairs will meet at the difference between their odds thus ascertained, i.e. A B will give C D thirty. Again, A, owing forty, and B, receiving thirty, meet C, receiving fifteen, and D, receiving two-quarters of fifteen. The strength of the pair A B is owed two-quarters, and that of C D receive three-quarters, and they will accordingly owe and receive those odds respectively. In neither of these cases are differential odds required. One more instance may, therefore, be given in which recourse must be had to the tables. A, receiving two-quarters, and B, receiving fifteen, have as a pair the strength of Class 3; C and D, receiving thirty and one-quarter and fifteen and three-quarters respectively, have the strength of Class 8; the difference between the odds of the two pairs would be fifteen and one-quarter, but a reference to the table shows that the odds required to be conceded by A B are fifteen and two-quarters. If all these players owed the supposed odds instead of receiving them, then by the agency of the differential table of owed odds they would meet on the terms of C D owing fifteen. This individual method of handicapping pairs is undoubtedly somewhat rough. It does not allow for the difference between men playing singly and in pairs, nor does it take account of the degrees of combined practice that a pair may have enjoyed. The arithmetical result will often require modification, but it at least provides some basis to work upon, and is therefore in my opinion safer than the rival method of classing pairs as such, which must generally be too conjectural to be trustworthy.

It may be observed that under the old system of bisques, the table from scratch to half-forty included sixteen classes, while the new tables, though calculated up to forty, include only twelve. From this it might be inferred that the old system admitted of more accurate adjustment of odds. But some of the old classes represented no real distinction, and the fluctuating value of the bisque in different hands and under different circumstances would of itself make this inference more than doubtful; and the variations of the standard of a man's play from one day to another are such as to make it probable that the division by quarters of fifteen is sufficiently close for all practical purposes, while it is almost certain that handicappers and players will prefer a classification that is uniform in operation and constant in value. A new and untried system will at first require on all hands patience and attention, and umpires must exercise great care to appropriate fractional odds to the prescribed games of a set; but it is conceived that the difficulty will not be found to be excessive, and although the new method is not by the Regulations made compulsory on the managers of prize meetings, an earnest hope may be expressed that in the paramount interest of uniformity all committees will loyally adopt it.

16

First Steps

First steps are proverbially difficult, and lawn tennis forms no exception to a rule that is, in fact, a condition of human nature. The difficulty of making them is, however, at least equalled by that of describing or directing them. To teach lawn tennis on paper is almost as hopeless as to teach swimming on a table. Excellence in a game, as in other things, is the product of natural aptitude and long and assiduous practice. There are, however, certain indispensable principles on the one hand, and certain natural but vicious habits on the other; and the observation of the former equally with the avoidance of the latter can to some extent be inculcated by precept. Strong natural aptitude amounts to genius, and is almost independent of instruction; long-established habit either is incapable of profiting by, or has outgrown the necessity for it. This chapter is intended, therefore, mainly for the ordinary beginner, who has neither acquired the one nor is gifted with the other; but if anyone after some practice finds that the ball struck by him does not travel at a fair pace, or that he has not adequate control over its direction, it is probable that his method is in some way unsound, and in that case he may without presumption be recommended to resume the study of first principles. Two physical qualities are necessary for lawn tennis as for other games – a good eye and activity – but the importance of each of these is often overrated. Nearly all English boys have played some game of ball; the eye and the hand have been to some extent trained to act together, and what is called a good eye, as distinguished from quickness of sight, which is quite a different thing, is principally the result of the acquisition of this habit. The same thing is to a great extent true of activity. Balls are reached in most cases, more by starting at once and in the right direction than by abnormal rapidity of movement. Let no young player be discouraged at the outset by the consciousness that he is not pre-eminently gifted by Nature in these respects. Both may to a great extent be acquired. Most people, however, are already possessed of sufficient eye to enable them to hit the ball; the difficulty is to hit it with effect, and for this the first requisite is to hold the racket correctly. On this point, there is no absolute uniformity in the practice of the best players, nor is there entire agreement among the writers on the subject. Dr Dwight urges strongly the extreme importance of being able to play a ball either forehanded or backhanded without changing the hold on the racket, on the ground that a change must require a certain amount of time and attention that cannot well be spared. He therefore recommends a method of grasping the racket that is intended to obviate the necessity of change. I cannot concur with this reasoning, and my convictions are strengthened by the great authority of Mr Wilberforce, who says, 'The time taken up by changing the grip is infinitesimal, and with practice becomes purely mechanical.' And again, 'I am firmly persuaded that with an unchanged grip there is less power of hitting, and, moreover, the racket is prevented from hitting the ball full, that is to say, without causing a twist.'

Now, the main object of modern lawn tennis is to meet the ball with a full racket, and though the accomplished player will on occasion deviate from this rule, it should be regarded by the learner as a law of the Medes and Persians. A short experiment will prove that there is no way of holding the racket unchanged for forehand and backhand strokes alike that will not seriously compromise the freedom of the player, especially if the ball does not bound exactly as he expects. For this reason, it is strongly recommended to the learner not to put himself into manacles by adopting the unchanged grip. Mr Wilberforce's advice is so sound and so clearly stated that it is impossible to improve on it, and it is, therefore, reproduced here verbatim :

> Take the racket in the left hand by the splice, the blade being vertical
> and the handle horizontal; then for the forehand stroke (the image
> on page 190 being a vertical section of the handle) the base of the

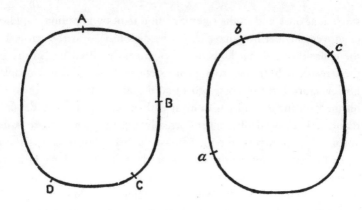

right hand will just overlap the butt; the knuckle of the thumb will be at A, the knuckle of the forefinger at B, the bend of the first joint of the forefinger at C, and of the second joint at D; the first joint will slope towards the blade, the other joints away from the blade; the thumb will slope very slightly towards the blade, its last joint jutting out from the handle; the first joints of the other fingers will lie across the handle at right angles.

For the backhand stroke, the knuckle of the thumb will be at A, the knuckle of the forefinger at B, and the bend of the first joint at C, the slope of the fingers will be exactly the same as in the forehand stroke; in fact, the change from the forehand to the backhand stroke is simply turning the hand back in the direction of the body, though rather more than a right angle. The racket should be grasped as firmly as possible if it is intended to make a severe stroke; it may be held more loosely for a gentle one.

The adoption of a right grasp of the racket is so important that drawings are appended (page 116) showing the hand and butt of the racket for the forehand and backhand strokes respectively, in order to make the relative positions of each clear to the eye as well as to the understanding.

But let the beginner remember that neither of these positions will come so naturally to him as to dispense with a good deal of trouble on his part. He will constantly find the racket slipping into a wrong position, and he should therefore at first make it his constant practice to satisfy himself that his hold is right before he prepares to receive the ball. After a time, habit will cause the racket to fall naturally into the right position for the forehand or backhand stroke, and he may then cease to think about it. Later on, he may – and if he ever becomes a good player he certainly will – change his hold according to the stroke he intends; but for the present, his watchwords should be 'forehand grip' and 'backhand grip', and, in familiar words, let him see that he gets it. The best way to secure this would be to induce a friend to toss a number of consecutive balls over the net to his forehand, and then a number to his backhand. When he has got fairly accustomed to take them consecutively, they may be alternated, and with care and attention, habit will make the change mechanical. In the absence of a friend sufficiently good natured, some writers recommend practice against a wall, now on one side, now on the other, and taking the ball at the volley and the half volley in succession, and afterwards combining all the varieties one after the other. This course will doubtless assist the learner to acquire readiness and accuracy; but he must remember that the ball will return from a wall at a different velocity and in a different manner from those it takes from the racket, and the court itself will therefore be the best as well as the most amusing school. The rudiments of one description of return mentioned by Dr Dwight may undoubtedly be acquired in this manner. A ball that has passed the player on his backhand is sometimes returned by bringing the right foot across and well behind the left, so that the body is turned almost to face the baseline; but this resource, though useful for extrication from a difficulty, is so much of the nature of a *tour de force*, that the beginner cannot be recommended to spend much time on its acquisition, though more advanced students may think it worthwhile to return to school in order to learn it.

To return to our tiro. As soon as he has learned to hold his racket correctly, and to alter his grasp instinctively when required, he must direct his attention to the attitude that he is to assume. The player should rest the blade of the racket upon the fingers of the left hand. He should stand with his body facing the net, so that a start may be made at once in either direction; his knees should be bent, his feet slightly apart and turned a little outwards, with the weight of the body resting on the toes rather than on the heels. The moment it is seen that the ball will come to the forehand, the left foot should be brought across and in front of the right, which will turn the body sideways, and the racket should be swung back to a greater or less extent according to the intended strength of the stroke. At the moment of striking, the weight of the body should be transferred from the right to the left foot, and the stroke will be stronger if this is accompanied by a short step forward with the left foot. Mr Wilberforce believes that accuracy is sacrificed by the forward step; on the other hand, it is certain that freedom is gained by it, and the weight of the body is more effectively and naturally thrown into the stroke in this way than by bending the knee only.

For the backhand stroke, the process is reversed. The right foot is brought across the left, the body faces to the left, and the weight is transferred from the left to the right foot. The engraving on page 117 illustrates the preparation for rather than the stroke itself, and the change of position has not yet been effected. The beginner should make it an invariable rule to take the ball when it is falling. He will see fine players occasionally deviate from this rule, and the time may come when he also will be able to do so with advantage; but for the present he will find that to take the ball falling not only gives him a longer sight of it, but also that it will go off his racket at a better angle, and will make a more effective stroke. Above all, let him meet it with a full racket every time, with no twist or cut, and as hard as he can without sending the ball out of court. He is not now playing a match. A few balls put in the net or out of court will cost him nothing, and it is easy to moderate his strength; while if he now falls into habits of timidity and the practice of patting the ball instead of hitting it, the difficulty of afterwards acquiring a strong stroke will be immensely increased.

With this view, he should endeavour to strike the ball with so much force that it shall drop between the service line and the baseline. If it drop nearer to the net than the former it is a weak stroke, and his opponent has comparatively little difficulty in crushing it or playing it away from him. If it drop close to the baseline, he will have a much longer sight of the return and greater choice of position, and, in addition to these advantages, it is always difficult to make a decisive stroke from a ball dropping in that part of the court. Let it be the constant aim, therefore, to make the ball drop as near as possible to the baseline. This is the most essential condition of good lawn tennis. No perfection of eye, no amount of activity, no skill in service or volley, will compensate for the want of what is known as a 'good length'. The beginner should therefore direct his undivided attention to the acquisition of a strong stroke, without allowing himself to be seduced by the charms of what may in comparison be called the accessories of the game – twist or cut, volley or half volley. When he has made himself master of a strong, unvarying stroke with a full racket, he may pass on to the acquisition of the luxuries of lawn tennis, because he will have ceased to be a beginner and will already be a formidable antagonist to ordinary players.

The following maxims may, however, be observed both now and even in later stages of progress:

1. Do not play too long at a time. About one hour every day, or two hours every other day, will be enough for most people. If the muscles are fatigued, the attention will be relaxed and faulty habits more readily acquired.

2. Always play your best, and, if possible, leave off when your interest in the game is insufficient to induce you to do your utmost.

3. Make yourself thoroughly acquainted with the laws of lawn tennis. Some good players do not know or are indifferent to them, and their play suffers in consequence.

4. Make it a rule always to observe the laws, and invariably play the strict game. If a beginner, for instance, is lax in the position of his feet for the service, it is probable that in his first match the umpire will remind him of his error in a manner very detrimental to his chance of success. Again, if he allows himself for the sake of convenience to stop a ball that would drop out of court, he will be not unlikely to continue the habit in matches.

5.   Take care that the net is the right height, and in marking out the court be sure that you have done so correctly. Length and elevation become by practice to some extent mechanical, and a very small deviation will put you out materially.

6.   Always assume that the ball will be returned. It is no excuse even to yourself, still less to your partner in the double game, to say, 'I thought it was not coming over'.

7.   Start at once for every ball. You will often start wrong, but practice will more and more correct this tendency, and the habit of quick starting, which can be acquired, will often take the place of activity, which is a gift of Nature.

8.   Do not try to deceive your antagonist. You will fail more often than you succeed, and the attempt will put you off your balance and will spoil your chance of attaining position for the next stroke.

9.   Play if possible with players better than yourself, taking odds sufficient to compel your opponent to do his best. You will thereby get better practice, and the gradual reduction of the odds will be a test of progress and a great encouragement to yourself.

10. Above all, watch good players: at first, in order to see how they stand, how they hold the racket and hit the ball; afterwards, in order to ascertain their position in the court, and to learn as much as possible of their tactics in play.

Some of these maxims are more or less applicable according to temperament and physical strength. Others are counsels of perfection that cannot in all cases be followed implicitly. It would be satisfactory were it possible to add yet one more to the list – always play with good balls on a good court; but civilization has not yet advanced far enough for a player to insist invariably on this condition without incurring, especially in the country, the imputation of conceit, churlishness or discourtesy.

17

Service

Assuredly it cannot be said of service in lawn tennis as it was in tennis, '*Le service, c'est l'ame du jeu*', nor will any lawn tennis player be able to give to an inquirer as to the varieties and quality of his service, the reply that is said to have fallen from an eminent French tennis player: '*Moi, Monsieur, j'en ai quarante-deux*'. To the wealth and abundance of the older game in this respect, the poverty of lawn tennis affords a striking contrast. It may have been a scoffer who defined service as 'hitting one ball hard into a net and dropping another gently over it', but it is certain that the monotony of this branch of lawn tennis is a defect in the game. Greatly as the actual strength and severity of service has grown during the last few years, it cannot be doubted that it was relatively more important in 1877, when, as we have seen, the proportion of games won by the server to those won by the striker out was about five to three. So great a preponderance as this could not be tolerated, and successive alterations of the service line have combined with greatly improved return to reduce the value of the service; and at the present moment it is a matter of doubt whether it is an advantage in a match between two even players to have the service. At all events, players whose service is not the weakest part of their game have often waived their privilege, not only to secure the better side, but for so small an apparent advantage as was until the recent change in the law derived from the delivery of service constantly from that end that is affected by sun or wind, in spite of the fact that in most matches a few services are delivered that are practically unreturnable.

For all service alike, the player must conform to laws 7, 8 and 9; and, in the four-handed game, to laws 32 and 33 also. Law 7 prescribes the position of the server. He 'shall stand with one foot beyond (i.e. further from the net than) the baseline, and with the other foot upon the baseline', otherwise it is a fault; but it is not now 'a fault if the server's foot, which is beyond the baseline, does not touch the ground at the moment at which the service is delivered' – an alteration, made in 1885, that has removed a frequent cause of faults.

The paucity of services has been mentioned; contrary to the usual formula, it is even more real than apparent. On paper, indeed, it is possible to make a list of varieties that is almost imposing. There are the overhand fast service; the overhand twist, given fast or slow and forehanded as well as backhanded; the reverse overhand twist; the horizontal service; the underhand twist forehanded and backhanded, which, like its overhand brother, may receive a reverse twist; and there are also some specimens of fancy service that are as varied and indefinite as was Mr Winkle's shooting. In practice, this ambitious array must be admitted to shrink to very meagre proportions. The real strength of lawn tennis in this department is centred in the hard overhand service, with which nearly every player commences, to which he is as constant as the exigencies of the game allow, and that he abandons only from fear of faults. Captious critics have often charged this particular service with the multiplication of faults, and the alleged waste of time consequent upon them; while some have even demanded that a single fault should count as a stroke. The result would probably be to deprive the service of its chief interest by driving this particular species entirely out of the field. If a ball could by possibility travel in a direct line from the racket to the ground, very few such services delivered by a man of ordinary stature could drop within the service line, fortunately it cannot travel except in a curve, and therefore some proportion of these services, delivered at full speed, escape the category of faults; but to do so they must drop within a margin of about two feet along the service line – a limit sufficiently narrow, and affording a strong argument against the abolition of the first fault.

Overhand Fast Service – In delivering the overhand fast service without any premeditated twist the first object is pace. The server will therefore naturally adopt such a position on the baseline, and such a mode of swinging the racket, as will most conduce to the attainment of the primary requisite. In regard to position, the toe of the front foot must be placed on the baseline and kept there until the ball has been struck. Some authorities recommend a short step forward, in order to throw the weight of the body into the service, but if law 7 is to be construed strictly, it may be doubted whether the server who makes a forward step can be said to 'stand' in accordance with the law. In any case, the forward step is dangerous, as the foot may not be placed precisely on the line, or the umpire, seeing the foot not to be there just before and immediately after the service, will almost inevitably be led to think that it never was there at all, and in either case a fault will be the consequence. The server may occupy any station he pleases on the baseline of his service half court. A position at or close to the corner of the court gives a longer diagonal, and the distance over which the striker out may have to travel in order to reach the ball is also somewhat greater; but these advantages are more than counterbalanced by the greater distance that the server himself will have to traverse in order to place himself in position for the next stroke, as well as by the fact that by serving from the corner he loses the chance of the very effective service down the centre line. It is usual, therefore, to deliver this service from the centre line, or about 2 or 3 feet to the right or left of it. The striker out should vary his position according to that of the server, having regard to the pace of the service and the state of the ground. If the service be delivered from the centre line, he will stand nearly, but not quite, behind the corner of the court, and a move by the server towards the corner will be met by a corresponding move to his own right or left by the striker out.

The next point is the swing for the service. The ball should be thrown gently up, nearly opposite to the right ear, to about the height to which the server can conveniently reach, and should be struck at its highest point just as it begins to fall. The body will sway slightly backwards and forwards once or more, the weight being transferred from one foot to the other till the moment of striking, when it will finally be thrown on the front foot, the other being generally lifted at the same time. The effect of the service will depend upon the accuracy with which it is timed. So far all players are agreed; but there is room for difference in regard to the swing. Some swing the racket directly backwards, so that when it is at its lowest point it is hanging behind the right shoulder. Greater speed can be obtained if it be swung much further back, so that at its furthest it is nearly horizontal, with the blade behind, or even projecting beyond, the left shoulder; but in this way it is more difficult to strike the ball with a full racket. In either case, the server should make ample use of his height and strike the ball at a point as high as he can conveniently reach. Unfortunately, the first service is not unfrequently a fault; the chief point then is to avoid a repetition of it. Most players make their second service almost the counterpart of the first, only modifying the pace, and endeavouring to make more accurate placing atone for want of speed. In this case, all attempt at the latter should be abandoned, and the attention directed solely to the object of making the ball drop as near to the service line as is compatible with absolute safety. It will be better, if possible, to serve to the backhand of the striker out, because few players are as strong backhanded as forehanded. Pace may be disregarded, because it is not more difficult, if indeed it be not easier, to return severely a moderately quick service of this kind than a slow one, while the latter certainly admits of more accurate placing. The server who has made a fault will find the overhand and underhand twist services to be useful alternatives to that now spoken of, and something may be said for them even as first services.

Overhand Twist – The overhand twist should generally be delivered from the corner of the forehand court, and if resorted to at all when the service is from the backhand court, it should be given from near the half court line. It is of little use against a strong player, its only merit being that, when delivered from the forehand corner, the twist of the ball will drive him outside his court, and so make it rather more difficult for him to attain position. When the ground is wet or slow, it will be found a useful variety. The attitude and swing are somewhat similar to those adopted for the overhand fast service, though much less swing is required, pace not being here the first object. The body is turned to face the sideline, the racket is grasped in a manner that is about midway between those recommended above for the forehand and backhand strokes, and at the moment of striking it is made to curl round the ball from right to left, holding it as long as possible. In this way, a very considerable twist from right to left can he imparted to the ball, while pace is still not altogether neglected. It is obvious that this right to left twist is much less effective from the backhand court, and for that reason this service when so delivered cannot be strongly recommended, except against an opponent who is slow on his feet, in which case a service of this kind made to drop close to the net is very effective, especially against a strong wind.

Horizontal Service – Another variety, useful more particularly from the left court, is the horizontal or cut service. The racket is not swung higher than the shoulder, and at the moment of striking it can hardly be too low, though it must still be kept horizontal by stooping the body. The face of the racket is quite open, and in striking passes along the under side of the ball, causing it to rotate vertically, and imparting to it much cut, accompanied generally by some lateral twist. For some reason difficult to explain, the ball on touching the ground will generally shoot more or less, particularly on a damp surface, and when such is the case it is useful, as well as for occasional variety; and it has the advantage of going to the backhand of the striker out, so that in the four-handed game, it has a tendency to separate the partners in such a way as to leave a default between them that may be useful at the next stroke. As a continuance, or against good players, it is for the most part of little use, and is only better than a mere toss.

Underhand Twist – The underhand twist is a more valuable but still rather uncommon resource. The desperate yet most judicious employment of it by Mr E. Renshaw, in 1883, at the close of his memorable match against Mr Lawford, is a remarkable proof of the occasional value of this service, which, so long as that match is remembered, will be retained in the armoury of lawn tennis players, though no one would dream of resorting to it habitually.

It should be delivered backhanded from the right and forehanded from the left court. In delivering it forehanded, the ball is dropped in front of the left foot, and is struck when about a foot or even less from the ground. The racket, held downwards, is swung almost vertically from right to left, and in the act of striking passes round the ball on its left side as though it were intended to cut a slice out of it. A great amount of lateral twist can thus be given, and the striker out is driven out of court, to the prejudice of his position; but it must be admitted that if the ball bounds at all high, a crushing return across the court is comparatively easy. The effect is assisted by a quick turn of the wrist in the act of striking, and, when delivered forehanded, the ball after the bound will break from left to right, while, if given backhanded, it will twist from right to left.

Reverse Overhand – The reverse overhand service is strongly recommended by Dr Dwight, and, as it has not been extensively adopted in this country, it is better to describe it in his own words. It is given in the

> same manner as the forehanded, except that the ball is thrown a little to the left of the head and farther forward than in the forehanded service. The racket passes in front of the face and round the ball from right to left.

The ball on bounding will break from left to right In regard to all these varieties, with the exception of the overhand fast service, it may be said that the value of them depends mainly on the judgment with which they are employed. In this, as in other parts of the game, the server should study the characteristics of his opponent's game, and the discovery of a weak point may guide him in the selection of service. He will not win many strokes against a good player directly by any of them; but indirectly, a well-chosen service will often conduce to the attainment of position, and ultimately to the winning of the rest. Even the overhand fast service will not be very frequently unreturned, and it is a question how far a player not specially gifted in this respect should make it his first object to deliver it at lightning speed. Dr Dwight recommends that he should do so even at the risk of many faults. Mr Wilberforce advises moderation in such a case. The safest rule will perhaps be to ascertain in practice what degree of speed is to the individual compatible with reasonable accuracy, and in matches to endeavour as far as possible to keep to that standard. Excessive temerity in endeavouring to force the pace will in this, as in most other competitions, lead to disaster, while timidity will leave the field open to a series of crushing repartees. The lines with which this chapter closes, altered in one word only from the original, indicate accurately enough what would have been the view on this subject of the short-sighted and indolent companion of our boyhood if he had devoted his attention to lawn tennis instead of to the art of poetry. The soundness of the advice may induce us to excuse the almost ostentatious avowal of his indifference to the art of the ball.

Sumite materiam vestris qui luditis aequam
Viribus, et versate diu quid ferre recusent,
Quid valeant humeri.

Which may be roughly translated:

Adopt a service suited to your strength;
If strong, hit hard; if not, give heed to length.

18

In Play

However much games may differ from each other, they have features of resemblance as well as points of divergence; and almost every game played with a ball has at least one fundamental principle that is common to all alike. It is this: that the weapon with which the ball is struck must be made to move in the same plane as the ball for as long a time as possible. In cricket, tennis, billiards and golf, this principle, variously expressed, is constantly insisted upon by the teacher, and its value is little if at all weakened by the fact that in two of them the object aimed at is moving, while in the others it is at rest. In the former case, its validity is enhanced by the possibility of a false bound, but it derives its principal force from the imperfection of human nature. No eye is absolutely perfect, no judgment perfectly infallible, and even were they so, no hand could be implicitly relied on to carry out the design of eye and judgment unerringly. But these considerations, weighty as they are in other games, have even greater force in lawn tennis, because on the truest turf the course of the ball is liable to be deflected by very slight inequalities, and, being much lighter than a cricket ball, it will be more affected by them. If a match could be played from start to finish on a lawn of the smoothness of a billiard table, the aberrations of eye, hand and judgment would still remain. If the racket is so held as to cross the flight of the ball, it is obvious that the time during which a stroke can be made accurately is extremely short; but this period can be made relatively long if the racket is so moved as to be, both before and after the moment of intended contact, at right angles to the flight of the ball. This possibility of prolongation more than any increase of speed has exercised a powerful influence on lawn tennis. It has dictated the orthodox grasp of the racket, it has modified the attitude of the player, and it has developed the most characteristic feature of lawn tennis by the creation of the 'drive'.

The Vertical Stroke – The elementary qualities of a good stroke off the ground have been already discussed, but this stroke forms so large a part of lawn tennis that it is necessary to go more into detail. It has been said that in most cases the ball should be taken when it is dropping, but it does not follow that this is to be done at one elevation only. In fact, there are two rival methods of striking the ball after it has bounded. For the first of these two methods, it is allowed to drop almost to the ground, and is then met with an almost vertical racket, at the moment when it is nearly but not quite opposite to the forward foot, which will of course be the left foot in the forehand, the right foot in the backhand stroke. At the moment of contact, the racket is frequently lifted, and the ball is in consequence made to rotate vertically in the direction of its flight. This lifting of the racket tends to lift the ball also over the net, and when the initial force is nearly expended, to bring it more quickly to the ground.

From this cause it is difficult to volley such a stroke well, but this is not all. The rotatory motion imparted to the ball causes it to leave the ground, after bounding, at a lower level and greater speed than it would have done had the racket not been lifted, and the difficulty of the return is increased by both these tendencies. This is, therefore, the lawn tennis stroke par excellence; it is possessed by almost every good player of the present day, and will be acquired more easily by imitation than by description. When made at high speed from the back or corner of the court, it is known as the 'drive'. It may be observed that in the woodcut the feet are rather too near together. The ball has perhaps come farther than the player consequence. An illustration of the attitude for the backhand drive is given on page 120.

The drive is the most brilliant and effective stroke of which the game is capable. The speed that can be imparted to the ball in this way must be seen to be believed, and a very small proportion of such strokes ever come back. It is hardly necessary to add that, like most other brilliant feats, they involve some risk of failure. Naturally, the whole class to which these strokes belong is available only when the

ball does not bound very high, and more frequently when the ground
is dead than when it is very lively. After long continued fine weather,
the bound is much higher, and many balls cannot be taken when they
are close to the ground. It is in such cases that there is brought into
play the second distinctive lawn tennis stroke.

The Horizontal Stroke – The ball is taken if possible nearly, but
not quite, at the top of its bound. The racket is kept at around the
level of the shoulder, the arm is rather stiff, and at the moment of
striking a slight turn of the wrist causes the racket to take hold of the
upper surface of the ball and to impart to it the same vertical forward
rotation as in the stroke last mentioned, with the same advantages
and the same increased speed after contact with the ground; and
with the additional merit that, as the ball need not be lifted over the
net, the curve is hardly perceptible, and interferes in even a smaller
degree with the pace. The invention of this stroke is attributed to
Mr Lawford, and forms a most valuable addition to the power of
attack. On one or other of these two principles, the large majority
of balls taken off the ground are returned. The horizontal stroke is
most applicable when the player is standing near to the service line,
or when the ball has dropped between it and the net, because no lift is
then required to surmount the latter, and the necessary pace can more
easily be imparted. A ball dropping between the service and baselines
is generally best returned by the underhand stroke, because at such a
distance from the net the curve required to pass over it is not violent,
but in many cases the choice depends upon the height of the bound.

In view of these two strokes, which, when seen at their best, are
simply the application of overhand cut to the ball, it may seem almost
paradoxical to say that the cut stroke is obsolete. Yet in the strict
sense of the word, this is the fact. In the early days of lawn tennis, a
few players had derived their training from a tennis court, and these
naturally adopted the practice of the game that was most familiar to
them. They knew that the attainment of a well and heavily cut stroke
was indispensable in the court, and they believed that it would be
equally effective on turf. Their main object, therefore, was to hold the
racket open or diagonally, to support the head, and to strike the ball
on the under side, so as to cause it to rotate vertically in the direction

contrary to that in which it was travelling, believing that a stroke thus effected would be more difficult of return than if made with a full racket. For the moment they were not disappointed. The stroke was unfamiliar to all but tennis players; the ball rose from the ground at an unexpected angle and many points were won and reputations achieved by this stroke alone. The textbooks of that day recommended the acquisition of a well-cut stroke to every beginner, and to increase its effect some even advised the use of an ordinary tennis racket, or at least of one made after its model with a very perceptible curve. But the difficulty in returning this stroke was soon found to be much exaggerated, and indeed to be in great measure imaginary. A singular instance of the extent to which even good players were at first puzzled by it, and of the rapidity with which they accustomed themselves to it, is afforded by a practice game played in 1880 at Wimbledon between Mr Lawford and Mr J. M. Heathcote, who had for many years been by far the best amateur tennis player of the day. Mr Lawford, though not so strong a lawn tennis player as he has since become, had at the time but two or three rivals. Mr Heathcote seldom played lawn tennis, and had enjoyed no opportunities of practice with the best performers; yet the cut service and stroke so puzzled Mr Lawford that for several games he missed stroke after stroke. All at once, as it were by intuition, he overcame the difficulty that had paralysed him; thenceforward his natural superiority reasserted itself, and, as might be expected, he easily defeated his opponent. The lesson that Mr Lawford mastered before one set had been completed was learned by inferior players, more slowly indeed, but not less surely. The cut stroke was robbed of all its terrors and most of its value, and for many years it has only occasionally been seen in good matches, for the most part when it is desired to place the ball with great accuracy at no great distance from the net, or when the ground or the balls are damp, in which case the latter will have a tendency to shoot. Mr W. Renshaw sometimes employs it on such occasions with great effect. The ball should always be taken when it is falling, and generally as low as possible. The employment of cut in what is called the horizontal service has been already discussed in dealing with that subject, and with these exceptions, the tennis cut has been discarded as tending to retard the progress of the ball, and may indeed be considered as obsolete, though a few elderly gentlemen who cherish the traditions of the past in remote and highly conservative districts still occasionally employ it with effect against very bad players and the average lady.

One other stroke from the ground requires to be mentioned, though it is not often seen, and still more rarely meets with much success. It sometimes is impossible to take the ball otherwise than on the rise, or to do so may be too great a sacrifice of position. In such a case there should be little or no swing, a fast-rising ball will inevitably go out of court if it be struck at and the racket should only meet it with the view of placing it as accurately as possible; but in any case this is a dangerous resource, and should be adopted on an emergency only.

For all strokes off the ground the player should endeavour to arrive in time to place himself for the return. Some degree of stability is necessary for an effective stroke, and though one or two players may be named who apparently do not object to take the ball on the run, they are the exception and not the rule. To start at once, to arrive in time, and never to be in a hurry, are three maxims that most men will do well to remember.

The Volley – Two of the three engines of attack available to lawn tennis players, the service and the stroke off the ground, have now been described; the third, and by no means the least important, remains to be considered. The volley has undergone more than one change since it made its appearance in the first tournament of 1877. It has been the subject of extravagant eulogy, and the object of unmeasured abuse. Uninjured by either extreme, it may be said now as then to be a good slave but a bad master. It consists of three varieties, two of which are as old as the game, while the third is, as we have seen, the invention of the Renshaws. There is first the purely defensive volley, practically a kind of lob, by which a dropping ball is met and returned high in the air to avoid the necessity of quitting position in order to make the return off the ground. Of this variety, the main object of which is to gain time, nothing need be said but that it should be made to drop near the baseline, and, as it must be very slow, it must be placed high enough to preclude the possibility of a crushing retort. The two other varieties are far more effective. Following as far as circumstances permit, the arrangement adopted in regard to service and stroke, volleys will be here divided into two classes – the overhand and the horizontal – a classification that, if not absolutely accurate, will be sufficiently intelligible. Almost all volleys delivered with any great degree of force will fall into the overhand category, while the horizontal will comprise nearly all those for which the racket is little if at all swung.

The Overhand Volley – The position for the overhand volley is in general close to the net. The arm may be bent at the elbow or fully extended upwards, and any degree of force may be employed, from a very moderate swing to the extent of letting the arm and the racket go after contact with the ball without any attempt to control either. This latter stroke is called a 'smash', and is fraught with danger to the unoffending parasols of ladies 30 yards off. The striker occasionally springs completely off the ground, and when the latter is lively, the ball can be made to bound over a pavilion at the end of the court. Such violence is seldom necessary, but the appreciation of the spectators generally proves that the brilliancy of the stroke atones for its extravagance. Many balls that do not admit of treatment so contemptuous can be disposed of quite as summarily, but with less expenditure of strength, by the overhand volley, either in the direction of the sidelines or straight down the court according to circumstances, and when made backhanded a moderate degree of force is advisable as being easier and less dangerous. The precise moment of striking depends on the distance of the striker from the net When he is close to it, he may employ a turn of the wrist to bring the racket more directly down on the ball than when he is further off, but in all cases, the weight of the body should be thrown into the stroke by a step forward, with the left foot for the forehand, and with the right foot for the backhand volley. The step forward is not confined to any one species, but is applicable to all alike, though it is more important when force is to be applied than when the racket is only moved gently forward to meet the ball. In most hard overhand volleys, the body and head are both thrown a little back, or even inclined sideways, so that the swing of the body as well as of the racket is thrown into the stroke. The smash is equally applicable to balls off the ground that drop short and bound high, but is hazardous from any position behind the service line.

The Horizontal Volley – Though the smash is particularly associated in the public mind with the name of Renshaw, it is the horizontal variety that may be more correctly said to be the creation of those gentlemen. The volley from the service – which must almost always be made with a horizontal – was introduced by them, and, in contrast to the older practice, is among the most distinguishing features of the lawn tennis of the day. The racket may be at a level much below the shoulder, or even close to the ground, in which case the player must stoop in making the stoke in order to lift it over the net, and will use but little force, though even then the ball should be hit and not allowed merely to bound off the racket. The head of the latter will be level with or above the elbow in all except very low balls. When the ball is at about the height of the shoulder, the elbow, shoulder and wrist should be free, the arm straightened at the moment of contact, and the racket will generally meet the ball full, though sometimes a little cut may be employed to keep the stroke under complete control, or when the striker is near the net, a dexterous turn of the wrist will place it in the exact spot required, whether across the court or otherwise. It is easier to volley such a ball backhand than forehand, and the reach is somewhat longer – a fact worth remembering when trying to pass a volleyer down the sidelines. When a ball comes down the sidelines at about the height of the net, an effective return along the same line may be made without the exertion of any force by bringing the racket out horizontally from the body. This Mr Wilberforce calls a 'push volley', and he advises that the wrist be kept stiff. He mentions another variety under the name of the 'drop volley', made within 3 yards of the net with a stiff wrist, the blade of the racket being vertical and drawn back just before contact with the ball, which will drop dead just over the net. Those who are familiar with Mr Chatterton's style of play will know better than from any description how this volley is made. A very telling stroke executed in perfection by Mr Lewis may be made when near the net by volleying the ball with a turn of the wrist across the court so as to drop near one of the sidelines.

Drive Volley – There is one other description of volley that is at present rarely seen but which may possibly be destined to a career of usefulness hereafter. When a lob is about to drop near the baseline, it is now generally returned either by the 'lob volley' mentioned above, which is a defensive stroke, or the player runs back and returns it again with a lob. In either case, he sacrifices the attack. There is no reason why such a stroke should not be returned hard by an underhand volley resembling the drive. The wrist should be kept very stiff, because otherwise the impact of the ball will force the racket down. With the 'push' and 'drop' varieties it forms an exception to the general rule as to the employment of the wrist, which in all other volleys is brought largely into play.

The Half Volley – The half volley is in strictness a stroke made by taking the ball at the moment when it is leaving the ground after bounding, but all returns made after the bound before a fresh sight has been obtained of the ball are commonly called half volleys. In neither case are they made by striking at the ball itself, but by a momentary calculation of where it ought to be. It is obvious that such a definition presupposes a very hazardous stroke. The authorities are unanimous in advising the beginner to omit it altogether from his consideration, and more experienced players to resort to it only when the stroke is otherwise hopeless. In most cases, it need not be made at all, a step forward converting it into a volley, while a step or two backward will make possible a far more certain and effective stroke off the ground. Nevertheless, it is a very fascinating resource, and in spite of moralisers will always be popular both with players and spectators. It is generally made with the racket held obliquely and with the arm extended. The further the racket is in advance of the striker, the more will it be inclined at an angle, and, as the ball must be rising at the moment of contact, the higher will be the return. If the ball is to be kept low, the racket may be turned over so that the upper edge is very slightly inclined towards the net, and the rise of the ball will still give it the necessary elevation. There are occasions, however, when the ball has passed the player. If it has done so to his forehand, he must cross the left foot over the right; if to his backhand, he must swing the right foot across the left and well behind it; and with his back to the net,

and with the racket approaching the vertical according to the distance
of the hall, he has a chance of making a 'gallery return'.

The Lob – The last of the methods of lawn tennis, the 'lob', is a
ball tossed high in the air, and, if possible, over the opponent's head.
It has been, and is, a most unpopular stroke, and has won its way to
general acceptance by its unquestioned utility. Its very name seems
to have been given to it in derision, for as a 'toss' it was known and
tolerated long before it was condemned as a 'lob'. Mr Hadow had
discovered its merits in 1878, and owed his victory over Mr Gore in
great degree to the discovery. It was, however, at that time used only
as an antidote to the man at the net, against whom even uncanonical
methods might be held legitimate. As play became gradually more
severe, it was adopted as a means of gaining time, and the respite
being the greater the higher the ball is tossed in the air, the lob rose
in altitude in proportion as its rank in reputation. It was soon found
that a very high toss is more difficult to volley as well as more easily
kept in court, and the additional fact that it is sometimes exceedingly
trying to the temper caused its unpopularity to keep pace accurately
with the frequency of its occurrence. The sense of the value of the
lob has, nevertheless, been continuously on the increase, and there is
no doubt at the present time that, not only as an occasional resource,
but as an habitual practice, lobbing is an integral part of the game.
Against a strong back player, ball after ball is played gently to the back
of the court in the hope of wearying the opponent, so that through
impatience or exhaustion he may hit the ball out of court or into the
net. Whether it be liked or not, the stroke must be recognised, and an
answer to it must be found. Let no man, therefore, despise the lob, but
let him remember that a short lob is the feeblest of possible strokes,
and the most certain to lead to disaster. It is very difficult to volley a
lob backhanded with effect; the stroke should, therefore, generally be
placed if possible to the opponent's backhand, but with a strong cross
wind it is impossible to observe this rule implicitly, and the ball must
be tossed to the windward side of the court. It may be unchivalrous
to lob persistently when the sun is in your opponent's eyes, but if the
object is to win a match, even courtesy may be carried too far. When
the ball must be returned from around the centre of the baseline, a lob

becomes the more useful because from that position it is very difficult to pass the enemy at the net on either side, and many balls that can just be reached, but so as to make a strong return difficult, may be safely lobbed. The worst feature of the stroke is that lobbing is apt to beget lobbing, and a long series of tosses would be wearisome alike to players and spectators. Still, there is no doubt that the resource is now too useful to be excluded, and the delivery of as well as the reply to it must be carefully studied. It may, of course, be lobbed back again, but this involves loss of position, and the better course is to volley moderately hard to the corner, and, if possible, the backhand corner of the court. In respect alike to the mode of lobbing, the occasion for it, and the answer to it, there is no better model than Mr E. Renshaw; but the player who shall first succeed in mastering the 'drive volley' above mentioned will not only have secured for himself a great advantage, but will also have dealt a death blow to lobbing on principle.

Every spectator must have observed that one player will appear to make his strokes with more apparent facility than another; and this comparative absence of effort is frequently attributed to the possession of quickness of eye or activity, and the result is called a graceful style. Grace is, of course, not to be made an object in itself. If studied or self-conscious, it will inevitably degenerate into artificiality or stiffness. To some fortunate individuals, it comes unsought; but it depends upon the perception, intuitive or acquired, of the principles upon which strokes ought to be made, rather than upon activity or upon a naturally graceful habit of the body. This perception, from whichever source derived, leads to the acquisition of what is now known as 'good form', or 'form' simply. This is quite a different thing from style. There are many styles of play: the ball may be taken high or low, with much or with little swing, on the run or stationary; and these differences are attributable to individual peculiarities, the elimination of which with reduction to one uniform and orthodox style, would be disastrous to the interest, the variety, and the beauty of the game. Yet, differing as they do in these respects, all good players display the characteristic known as 'form', and a few words may be devoted to the explanation of what it is. It is the art of so moving, so carrying the body, and so wielding the racket, as to produce the greatest possible effect with the least possible waste of force, or, as Dr Dwight terms it, 'the least friction'. It is possible to make extraordinary strokes from extravagant attitudes, and such *tours de force* are necessary on emergency; but even in such cases the preservation of the balance is important, because it conduces to a quick start after the stroke has been made. Nothing is so destructive of the balance as long strides. With short steps, the balance of the body is never lost, and it is much easier to start quickly in a required direction. The player should try, therefore, to keep his feet under him, and when at rest (which he very seldom should be) to divide his weight nearly equally between them, and upon the toes rather than the heels. At the moment of striking the weight is always on the foot that has made the last step. The other foot will sometimes be in the air, but even then it must never appear to be left behind, but be ready either in its turn to become the pivot or to start quickly back again. There should be no useless flourish, and the racket should generally be carried through the stroke without any check at the moment of contact with the ball. The preliminary swing, on the other hand, is more often in excess than in defect of the required amount. These are the principal essentials to good form; some or all of them are exemplified in each of the illustrations appended to this and the preceding chapter, and careful observation of first-rate play will impress their value still more strongly on the mind.

These five strokes – the service, the stroke off the ground, the volley, the half volley, and the lob – are the weapons in the armoury of the lawn tennis player. The acquisition of some familiarity with each of them, except the half volley, should be the first object of the beginner so soon as he has passed from first principles to the study of the game itself. The advanced player, if he aspires to excellence, must seek to make himself master of them all. If he can succeed so far as to hit as hard and as accurately from the baseline as Lawford, place his hard hits and smash like W. Renshaw, lob as well as E. Renshaw, and volley like E. W. Lewis – especially if to these qualities he can add Hamilton's activity and certainty – he will not only be the best player of his day, but he will also be not far from perfection, so far as we can at present conceive of it. All-round play is the great secret of eminence, and it is because Mr W. Renshaw combines excellence in all these strokes in a higher degree than anyone else that he has been able to attain and retain so long the first position among lawn tennis players. It is obvious, however, that such versatility is not to be acquired rapidly. Every player will find that natural aptitude will have a tendency to force him into a certain groove, though this tendency will be strengthened or modified by the habits of those with whom he most frequently plays. He will be by preference a back player or a volleyer, he will volley from the net or from the service line, trust much or little to his service, and lob by choice or only on compulsion, according as his own powers or those of his friends may happen to influence him. It is useless to speculate whether good back play can beat good volleying, or whether the volley from the net is superior to that from the service line. The time has gone by for such experiments. The discovery that the all-round player is the best player was made by Mr Hartley in 1883, and the certainty of its truth has been confirmed by the experience of every year. The best advice that can now be given to a player who aspires to the first flight is this: If you are exceptionally strong at the volley, devote yourself for a time in practice almost exclusively to back play. Should the lob or the service be below the general standard of your play, give especial pains to the acquisition of these strokes. Bring the weakest of them, if possible, up to the level of the strongest, so as to raise them all to a uniform degree of excellence as near to perfection as your powers of body and mind admit.

19

Tactics of the Single Game

Early controversialists asserted with much persistency a fancied analogy between lawn tennis and rackets. This must now, at least, be admitted to have been based on a confusion between three things widely different in their nature – principles, methods, and tactics. In its principles, lawn tennis is the true child of tennis, bearing but little resemblance to games of another family; and it is distinguished broadly from rackets by the dividing net. In respect of method, however, lawn tennis owes but little to its parent. It is hardly too much to say that a tennis player's first endeavour, if he wish to excel at lawn tennis, should be to unlearn all the traditions of his court. The diagonal racket, the constant injunctions to 'support the head', the carefully inculcated attitude, must all be discarded as useless if not absolutely hurtful. Even the word 'position' has received a new interpretation – it no longer means the attitude in which the ball can lie struck with greatest effect, but the part of the court from that the attack may most effectively be made. As regards method, a resemblance does exist between rackets and lawn tennis, particularly in the manner in which the ball should lie struck. In tactics, lawn tennis is original and is little beholden to tennis, rackets or any other game, except that in four-handed tennis, as in lawn tennis, a stroke straight down the middle of the court between the two partners is a frequent and effective resource. The tactics of the single game have grown up with its development, and the principles upon which they are founded are the simple result of observation, experience and common sense. The title prefixed to this chapter might, of course, be held to include the promulgation of an entire code of elaborate instructions as to the employment of the different strokes that have been discussed in that which preceded it. Directions might be given as to the occasions when the stroke should be made down the sideline, and when it should be struck across the court, or as to the advantage in particular circumstances of adopting the drive or the lob. No attempt of this kind will here be made, or, at least, it will be confined within very narrow limits. Such directions may be useful in other games, where the nature of the attack dictates more or less rigidly that of the defence; but in lawn tennis this is not the case. It hardly ever happens that a particular stroke is obviously appropriate to the exclusion of all others. The position of the striker and that of his opponent, the strength or weakness of either, the conditions of weather, wind and sun, with a host of other considerations, must all be included in the calculation, so that the best tactics are those that may be expected to lead up to a decisive coup, and not a succession of strokes that, taken one by one, may be considered to be ideally the best. This view of the meaning of tactics in lawn tennis does not, however, exclude the enunciation of certain principles that are now firmly rooted in the practice of good players. The first of these principles is almost a truism, and will be self-evident to everyone who has seen one or two public matches or good games. It is this: Every player has a favourite spot in the court that represents to him the best 'position', whether for attack or defence, from which he departs as seldom as possible, and to which he will always return when the exigencies of the game have driven him from it. This spot is not the same for all players. Some will by preference place it on the baseline or behind it, others at or about the service line, or even nearer to the net. It is never very far from the half court line, and may be almost anywhere on it, except that the space between the service and baselines is the worst part of the court for all purposes. It follows that one great tactical aim of the player is to secure the position for himself, and to force his opponent from it. To do this he must, so far as possible, play the ball away from the enemy by placing it either across the court to the corners, down the sideline, across the court to the sidelines, or over his rival's head to the baseline. Which of these expedients he will adopt, or whether he will resort to the hazardous experiment of trying to drop the ball close to the net, is a question no rules will solve, depending, as it does, on the circumstances of the moment.

The habitual position of a player is not, however, that from which he generally delivers the finishing stroke, except when the rest is concluded by a mistake on the part of one or other of the players, or in the case of the consistent back player who trusts to sheer force and pace alone. Such players are now few in number, and the majority of rests are terminated by a hard volley from the vicinity of the net. It is obvious that the player whose ordinary position is near the service line has an advantage in this respect over the baseline player, from the shorter distance he will have to cover. The second great tactical principle is, therefore, to manoeuvre for the position that will give the first chance of finishing the rest. For this purpose, the opposite player should be kept at or forced to retreat to the baseline; he should be worked from side to side of the court, if he runs up he should be driven back by a lob, and as soon as he has been forced back beyond the baseline, or quite outside of the court, and generally not till then, there is a chance to go up and finish the rest. The great secret of success is not to be in a hurry to run up. Many players, especially service line volleyers, do so immediately after the delivery of a fast service; but this is open to the objection that such a service puts the server off his balance, and some time is required to get into position after it. Moreover, a fast service will often be returned at nearly equal speed, and a player running up at once is very apt to be passed. If, however, he should find that he has run up prematurely, let him go back if there is time; if not, he must trust to the chapter of accidents, and to his own quickness and resource. It is a very dangerous experiment to go up after a weak second service; the safer plan is to assume position about a yard behind the baseline, or further back on a hard ground, and to wait for a better opportunity.

To receive the first service, the striker out should stand with his right foot on an imaginary prolongation of the sideline, much or little behind the baseline, according to the hardness of the ground; a little further to the right in the forehand court, to the left in the backhand court, if the service be delivered from the corner. As the majority of services will come to the backhand of a player in this position, he is recommended to hold the racket with the backhand grip. After a fault he will move forward a little into the court, and, as he will have more time for consideration, he can place himself so as to receive the service forehand. The return from the right court of the service may be either down the sideline or across the court. If it be the former, the striker out should generally go up to volley, and if an attempt be made to pass him on his forehand, he will have the option of volleying across the court, so that the ball may drop as close to the net as possible, or back along the same sideline. If his opponent tries to pass him on the other side, he will have a similar choice, or if the return be a lob, he should volley it hard into the opposite corner. But the service may have been returned hard across the court, so that the ball has dropped near the sideline, between the service and baselines. In this case also the striker out may follow up his stroke, taking care at the same time to be prepared for the contingency of a lob or of a return along the sideline. The same principles apply to the return of the service from the left court. It is easier to start quickly after receiving than after delivering the service, and the striker out may, therefore, with less imprudence than the server, run up to the net; but if he has made a feeble return he will do better to remain at the back of the court. It may be worth mentioning that while a weak volley is in most cases a present of the stroke, a gentle cross volley well placed near the sideline is as good, and often better, than a hard one down the court. Certain strokes may be placed in a kind of Index Expurgatorius, as altogether unfit for use when there is any alternative. Among these are a gentle return down the middle of the court, a short lob, a weak volley and any slow ball placed within reach of a volleyer at the net; but a fast ball straight at him is sometimes effective enough, and may be the best way out of a difficulty. If it is a matter of choice whether the attempt to pass a volleyer at the service line shall be made to his forehand or backhand side, it is worth remembering that it is in general easier to pass him on his forehand and by a stroke across the court than by one down the sidelines, but if the player is quite at the back, a lob is usually the safer resource.

A considerable part of what may fairly be called tactics has no reference to the use of particular strokes, but relates either to the preliminaries of the match or to the general lines on which it is fought. The best back play, for instance, is heavily handicapped on a wet court, or if it be otherwise in a bad state; and the all-round player has then the great advantage of being able to accommodate himself to the conditions of the moment. A previous inspection of the ground is a profitable investment of time, to ascertain its peculiarities and any superiority that one end may have over the other. If there be a marked difference between them, the right to change at the prescribed times, instead of at the end of the set, must be claimed before tossing for choice. Otherwise it will be too late to do so, and ends can be changed only in the odd set.

It is not, however, always in his interest to change. Of two players, the one who thinks himself the better should make the claim, and he who thinks himself the worse should abstain from it. The former should, as far as possible, exclude luck, the latter should embrace every chance of getting it on his side. In a good court, the position of the sun and the direction of the wind ought to be the main considerations affecting choice, but the nature of the background may make one end better than the other; and service being now generally regarded as no advantage between equal players, the winner of the toss should choose the best end, taking note in doing so not only of the position of the sun at the moment, but of what it will be in the course of the match. So long as the players were allowed to change sides every game, the advantage of winning the toss was reduced to a minimum, and the arrangement of the service, which was necessarily delivered from the same side throughout, became of greater importance. Ingenious devices were therefore resorted to by the winner of the toss to secure the delivery of the service from such court as might seem to be to his interest; but the loser of the toss could dictate the end from which the service should come, and on this account it was often a positive disadvantage to win the toss. This defect is now remedied by requiring the change to be made, if at all, after 'the first, third, and every subsequent alternate game of a set', so that service is delivered about equally from either end. Moreover, the winner of the toss can now compel his opponent to make the first choice. Something may be learned of the enemy's play beforehand, and something also picked up in the course of the preliminary 'knock-up'. When playing against a strong antagonist, and especially in a handicap, the weaker should play a hard, fast game. Some luck is sure to fall to his share, and, at all events, a weak game is of no use against such an opponent. The latter will be compelled to play a quieter game than usual if he has to concede long odds, and must, therefore, also give many opportunities to kill the ball. With this exception, a man should endeavour to play his usual game in a five-set match, and to maintain it steadily from the beginning to the end. He will want all the endurance he possesses, and many matches have been lost, and still more jeopardised, by an initial effort too great to be sustained. On a similar principle it is unwise for a player to drop his game, unless it be absolutely necessary to do so. It is proverbially difficult to pick up a dropped game, and the increased confidence derived from temporary success will sometimes make it impossible. It may, of course, occasionally be judicious to let a set go when victory is hopeless, but this course should be resorted to but rarely and with extreme caution. In a three-set match, it is allowable to play a faster game, the effort being proportioned to its duration.

It is not the usual practice of lawn tennis players to submit to strict training. After the season has commenced, few of the regular match players have much chance of being otherwise than fairly fit for hard work. Some players do more in the way of preparation than others. Mr E. Renshaw is supposed to do rather less, yet no one has exhibited more wonderful proofs of endurance; but his practice in this respect will not be safely imitated by everyone. Those who have not yet fully gauged their own powers will do well to remember that a tournament extending over several days, on each of which it is possible that five advantage-sets may be played, is one of the severest tests of constitutional soundness and physical strength to which men have ever voluntarily subjected themselves in the pursuit of a game. It must tax the strongest man severely, and the apparent inequalities of form exhibited by the same player on successive days, as well as the startling changes of fortune that the course of a single match will sometimes display, are in great measure attributable to the severity of the exertion. The most experienced players find it occasionally necessary to allow a set to go by default, in order to secure a short breathing space or to restore their temporarily exhausted energy; and they have done this though it is notorious how hard it is to recover a dropped standard of play, and how dangerous it always is to give to an antagonist any encouragement. Still more in accordance with sound policy is it occasionally to leave alone a stroke that can only be returned by a violent effort, and then only by so feeble a return as to leave no hope that the next will not be decisive. In such a case, success may cost more than the stroke is worth, and it may be prudent to let the ball alone altogether. Nevertheless, the fact that strokes, games and sets are sometimes discreetly allowed to go by default is a proof that a long and hard match is no child's play, and that want of condition will show its results at an early stage.

But when the last word has been said on the subject of skill, judgment and endurance, moral qualities must still be admitted to have a determining influence upon the issue. Of these, a player will find confidence in himself to be one of the most important. There are few games in which the form of players varies so much from day to day. One who has been seen playing brilliantly on one occasion, will within a day or two perhaps display a very moderate exhibition of skill. A piece of bad luck will in one case discourage effort, in another it will intensify the determination to win in spite of it. Temperament has much to do with these inequalities. One man can play his best when he has slightly the best of the handicap, another requires a shade of odds against him to draw out his powers to the utmost. A singular instance of this idiosyncrasy occurred at Cannes early in 1886. Each of two well-known players, Mr R. U. Sears, the American champion, and Mr W. C. Taylor, believed that he could give the other odds. Two matches were played, each alternately giving the other half fifteen, with the curious result that in both cases the giver of the odds won the match; but it is clear that neither player can have displayed his true form in both matches. In addition to such oscillations as these, it is the fact that no game is more trying to the temper than lawn tennis, and in none is the loss of it more apparent to the spectators or more disastrous to the individual. In cricket, the bowler may free his mind by unusual pace in the next ball, or the batsman may play the part of Achilles in the pavilion for half a day without attracting special notice; but unnecessary violence, apathy or petulance in a lawn tennis player is visible to everyone, and many times important matches have been lost by the not unnatural impatience caused by an egregious piece of bad luck or an erroneous decision. Such accidents are bound to occur, and should be discounted beforehand. The cultivation of an even temper and a fixed determination not to be put out are among the most important elements of success.

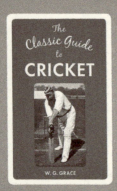
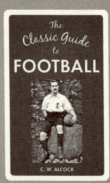
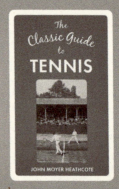
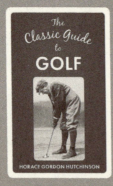